Plowing in Hope

Plowing in Hope

Toward a Biblical Theology of Culture

David Bruce Hegeman

Canon Press

MOSCOW, IDAHO

David Bruce Hegeman, *Plowing in Hope: Toward a Biblical Theology of Culture*

© 1999 by David Bruce Hegeman
Published by Canon Press, P.O. Box 8741, Moscow, ID 83843
800-488-2034 / www.canonpress.org

05 04 03 02 01 00 99   9 8 7 6 5 4 3 2 1

Cover design by Paige Atwood Design, Moscow, ID

Cover art: Grant Wood (1892–1942), *Fall Plowing*, 1931, oil on canvas, 29 1/4 x 39 1/4 in.; Deere Art Collection, Moline, Illinois

Printed in the United States of America.

ISBN: 1-885767-63-3

Thanks to *The BIAS Report* for permission to reprint what appears in the present work as the appendix. It originally appeared as an article titled "Toward a Christian Vision in the Arts" in *The BIAS Report*, May 1991.

To Marjorie, my wife—
faithful culture-maker and cultivator
of our four thriving olive plants

Contents

There are two principal strands of human history: culturative history and redemptive history.

Culturative history is God's unfolding purpose for man, in which mankind plays a chief role in the development and transformation of the earth from garden-paradise to the glorious city of God.

Culture is the concretization—the rendering in some permanent form—of mankind's culturative acts, commonly manifested in man-made objects, structures, texts, etc. Such artifacts stand apart from but (ideally) work in harmony with God's natural creation or "nature."

Culture is an essential outworking of mankind's unique place within God's creation as image-bearer of God. Man's cultural activities grow out of his special relationship to the earth (*adam*/*adamah*) to work and keep it. Man is commanded to utilize his innate skills to develop the potentialities "hidden" in the earth waiting to be discovered and realized.

The scope and richness of God's culturative program for man implies and necessitates the involvement of a community of people with varied functions and abilities. Differentiation and specialization in culturative tasks are inescapable as societies mature and will normally lead to a governing order and a cultural elite.

Culture manifests itself in varying degrees of expressive intensity, formality, and seriousness. "High" culture generally designates those cultural artifacts self-consciously made for lasting use as objects of intellectual and/or aesthetic contemplation, or for religious veneration/service. "Low" culture designates objects made for common purposes, with a special focus on utility.

PREFACE

This book grew out of a pair of adult Sunday school classes I taught at Cascade Presbyterian Church in Eugene, Oregon, in the Spring of 1997. I had been invited to speak there by then intern (now Pastor) Jason Dorsey, with whom I had conversed on numerous occasions in the preceding months about our mutual love for the Reformed Christian faith and about its relationship to the arts and contemporary culture. Jason, as coordinator of the adult classes at Cascade, invited me to do a brief series on the topic of Christianity and Culture. At first I was a bit daunted at this task, since my real passion was the study of the relationship between the Christian faith and the visual arts and aesthetics. I had spent some time before, studying the Bible's teachings on culture-making, but only insofar as it formed the backdrop to Christian involvement in the arts. In the course of organizing my thoughts on the topic at hand, I came across the idea of setting forth the biblical doctrine of culture in terms of ten propositions (following loosely the example of Peter Berger's classic work on capitalism). The class went well and several people commented positively on the propositional format. It occurred to me that the propositions might make an excellent outline for a book. With Jason's kind encouragement I began the task, taking his wise advise to keep the text brief.

I would like to thank Jason, Pastor Jack Davidson, and the session of Cascade Presbyterian Church for allowing me the opportunity to participate in their adult Sunday school series. The discussion we had during and after the two classes was lively and challenging and contributed to much of the shape of this volume. This book was also vastly improved by those friends of mine who read some or all of it in its various stages and gave me their candid comments and suggestions. For this I would like to thank Pastors Jason Dorsey and William Renkema, Professor David Ayers, Jan Cohen, and most of all, my wife Marjorie, whose wise, positive criticism made my approach much more balanced and practical. While all these dear brothers and sisters helped me with the manuscript, I take sole responsibility for the finished product and any errors or blunders it might contain. Lastly, I would like to extend a hearty thanks to Doug Jones, Canon Press, and the elders of Community Evangelical Fellowship in Moscow, Idaho, for allowing this project to become a published reality.

David Bruce Hegeman
Dallas, Oregon
September 1999

INTRODUCTION

"You are a man of culture."

—fortune cookie message
received by the author

The industrial valley of Cubatão, twenty-five miles southeast of São Paulo, Brazil, is reputed to be the most polluted place on earth. Free of all governmental regulations and business scruples, dozens of chemical factories, steel mills, and manufacturing plants belch tons of lethal fumes into the air and continually pour various toxins into the nearby estuary. Such unmitigated dumping into the environment has taken its toll. The surrounding hills, once covered with lush vegetation, now lie bare, punctuated here and there by the open scars of erosion. The river, once teeming with fish, is now an icy-black pool of death. It is as if William Blake's "dark Satanic Mills" have become a terrifying reality.

Nearly 12,000 miles away on the other side of the earth stands the magnificent Phoenix Hall *(Hōodō)* of the *Byōdō-in* Buddhist temple in Kyoto, Japan. Originally a palace, the main building is composed of an elaborate network of hand-carved timbers and interlocking brackets which hold up massive, cantilevered tile roofs. Supported on stilts, the whole structure seems to float as if it were weightless. On a still spring day when the cherry blossoms are in bloom, the view of the temple across its reflecting pond is said to be ravishingly beautiful. It is a paradigm of peace and inner harmony—the Buddhist ideal.

Whether beautiful or repulsive, uplifting or destructive, the effects of human habitation are everywhere to be seen across the whole surface of the earth. We call these durable effects of human habitation "culture." Culture is the output of all human societies, the product of deliberate human activity. Wandering nomads, small agricultural communities or megalopolises—people in all situations throughout all history have made artifacts. These include texts (written or handed down orally), objects (tools, vessels, clothing, art objects, etc.), and structures (from fences to roads, grass huts to towering cathedrals). The intricate network of artifacts, and the activities and rituals which go into making them, form a society's culture, no matter how primitive or sophisticated.

As Christians, we must never assume that culture "just happens" (the evolutionary view). Rather, as believers of God's holy Word, we must assert that since "the LORD has established His throne in heaven, and His kingdom rules over all" (Ps. 103:19), "there is a time for every purpose and for every work" (Eccl. 3:17; cf. 3:1) which is determined and controlled by God (Is. 46:9–10; Dan. 4:35). Human beings are a part of God's creation and are therefore under His divine rule. Made deliberately in God's image (Gen. 1:27), men and women are inescapably intelligent, verbal, moral, and creative beings. How this plays out in man's cultural endeavors will be explored in detail in part 1 of this book.

The breadth and diversity of human culture is astounding, reflecting the glorious superfluity of the Father's magnificent creation. As God creates, so humans make. Our works are never as stupendous as the Father's, yet they are still of great value. Tragically there is another dimension to the diversity we find in human cultural expression which goes beyond differences in style, temperament, utility, and type. There is the effect of sin. We see this played out in the horror of Cubatão. Since the fall of Adam we have rebelled against our Creator and our divine image has been distorted (but not destroyed). We still think and speak and will and make, but now, instead of glorifying God in all that we do, we conspire and curse and hate and destroy. Culture continues to exist but in ugliness and dissonance with the original good creation. Yet somehow there are artifacts which have some apparent good. We see the splendor of the Phoenix Hall—the product of an unbelieving Buddhist culture—and wonder how something so beautiful can be built for such an ugly end. Yet it is so. In part 2 of this book we will examine the effect of sin on creation and culture-making, and explain how it is possible that non-Christians can make useful artifacts and what their place is in God's plan. And we will explore the relationship between God's redemptive purpose to save human beings and their culture-making. But first we will examine the definition of culture in some detail, provide a preliminary overview to culture's place within the Bible, and briefly outline the Church's historic response to culture.

BACK TO THE ROOTS

The word *culture* has come to take on a number of diverse meanings. One recent reference book defines culture as "the beliefs, behavior, language, and entire way of life of a particular time or group of people." This, the most broad definition of the term, corresponds to a common use of the term in the field of anthropology. The definition continues, "The term also may have a more specific aesthetic definition and can describe the intellectual and artistic achievements of a society." Hence, we commonly speak of a "cultured" person as one who is well versed in literature and the fine arts—a connoisseur. Herein lies the clever irony of the fortune cookie message quoted at the start of this section. According to the broad definition of culture, it reads as a tautology: *all* men are men of culture by definition! Read according to the second definition, the message is sly flattery. One is tempted to respond, "Well, thank you for recognizing my extraordinary personal virtues in this area . . ." No doubt this kind of missive sells a lot of Chinese food!

The word *culture* is derived from the Latin *cultura*, which is the past participle of the verb *colere*, meaning *to plow or till.* *Cultura* was normally used in agronomic contexts to denote the cultivation—the active care or tending—of plants or animals. Hence we speak of agri-*culture* as the care of the soil to grow crops (*agros*=field, in Greek). The term could also be used in a religious context to mean *worship.* The idea here seems to be that in the same way the farmer actively fusses over his crops, so the worshiper gives rapt attention to the deity he serves. Thus the term is closely related to the Latin *cultus* meaning *adoration* or *veneration*. The English language retains this connection with such terms as *cult, cultic, occult*, etc.

According to the *Oxford English Dictionary,* the word *culture* was not introduced into the English language until the fifteenth century, via Old French. Originally it was used strictly in the agricultural sense, with a special focus on breeding (husbandry). It was not until the following century that the term began to be used in the figurative sense to describe the development of the mind: rendering improvement or refinement by education or training. Farming was used as a metaphor for the educational process. Thus Thomas Hobbes spoke of the education of children as "a culture of their minds." By the 1800s (when the ideals of Enlightenment humanism had taken hold of Western society) the term *culture* came to mean *the state of being refined in mind, tastes, and manners, and to the intellectual side of civilization* (corresponding to the second definition of culture cited at the beginning of this section). Matthew Arnold, an outspoken proponent of this idea of culture, is often quoted as stating that culture is "the acquainting ourselves with the best that has been known and said in the world."

By the end of the nineteenth century, culture began to be used to denote more generally the whole way of life of a group or society, not just its better achievements (corresponding to the first definition of culture cited in this introduction). This can be called the anthropological sense of culture. At first a vestige of the agricultural metaphor of growth was retained. The older, Arnoldian idea of culture became "high" culture, aboriginal societies were referred to as "primitive" cultures, the Western middle class was referred to as "low" culture, etc. But as anthropology came to embrace a more egalitarian, relativistic outlook, there was a corresponding insistence that all cultures were equally legitimate and should be valued as such. At this point the agricultural metaphor was lost; there was no difference to be seen in the societal equivalents of seedlings and mature, fruit-bearing plants.

Such a cultural outlook is sharply opposed to the inescapable culturative order of growth and development established by God in creation. I will therefore argue in part 1 of this book that the

Bible implicitly, yet unequivocally, teaches that: (1) there is (and ought to be) real cultural development; (2) occupational differentiation and societal stratification are necessary in order to meet God's command for global cultural development; and (3) some artifacts are recognized as having greater value because they are more intellectually and aesthetically refined and made with greater skill. Cultural egalitarians tacitly recognize this difference every time they use a word processor to compose one of their anarchistic essays (rather than using a typewriter or writing it out longhand) or take pleasure in a glass of fine imported wine.

While I readily agree with the definition of culture as the overall way of life of a given human society (including both its common *and* intellectually advanced elements), the view of culture used in this book will focus on culture as a concrete phenomenon. As Henry Van Til proposes, culture is "the secondary environment which has been superimposed upon nature by man's creative effort." Thus I define *culture* as *the product of human acts of concretization undertaken in the developmental transformation of the earth according to the commandment of God.* I favor viewing culture in this way because this definition highlights culture as a specific class of actions human beings perform upon God's original creation. A real change must take place on the earth or culture has not occurred. Culture is not an activity to keep mankind occupied until something else (presumably better) happens. It has a particular God-ordained end in view: the development of the earth into a global network of gardens and cities in harmony with nature—a glorious garden-city. Moreover, the process of cultural development has a basic temporal/progressive aspect: later cultures build upon and utilize the insights, technology, motifs, etc., of antecedent cultures as an important part of their cultural endeavors. This can only take place if artifacts from earlier cultures are somehow known or continue to exist. The more ephemeral aspects of a culture are not necessarily less important or less valuable, but if lost, they cannot make an impact on subsequent human societies.

Henry Van Til is credited with coining the aphorism *culture is religion externalized.* We must be careful how we interpret this phrase. If we assume by these words that religion is an internal, private affair which occasionally becomes externalized when it

interfaces with culture, we have missed the point. Our Christian
faith is to affect all areas of our life in obvious, overt ways
(Matt. 5:13–16). Van Til was describing an inevitable process:
artifacts necessarily reveal the worldview of the individual or group
who makes them ("by their fruits you will know them"—
Matt. 7:20). Thus culture is the concrete expression of a society's
religious and philosophical commitments; it flows out of the
heart—as it were—of the society which produces it (Prov. 4:23).

BIBLICAL TERMINOLOGY

Culture is in evidence throughout the pages of Scripture. Nearly
every page speaks of farming or buildings or singing or commerce
or religious rituals or the like. In fact, the Bible is itself a product
of culture. The Bible is both fully the Word of God and fully the
writings of human authors. As the Word of God, Scripture is
over culture and offers an infallible, perfect standard by which all
cultures are to be judged and evaluated. Yet as texts authored by
believing human beings providentially prepared and moved by
the Holy Spirit (2 Pet. 1:20–21), these works flow out of the
cultural language, perspective, customs, idioms, and literary forms
of the society from which they emerge. The inescapability of
culture was no less true for the covenant community of the Old
and New Testaments.

While the Bible has a great deal to say about culture (indeed,
this book purports to be a *biblical theology* of culture), curiously,
the Bible has no Hebrew or Greek equivalent for the English
term *culture*. (The word *culture* does not appear in most English
translations of the Bible.) The closest term in the NT Greek is
the word *ethos*, which is usually rendered *custom* or *habit*. It is
used in the NT to refer to the religious customs or traditions of
the Jews (Luke 1:9; 2:42; John 19:42; Acts 6:14; 15:1; 26:3;
28:17); to the customs of societies outside the covenant
(Acts 25:12); or to one's personal "customs" (i.e., habits:
Luke 4:16; Acts 17:2; Heb. 10:25). As such, *ethos* refers to the
normal way of doing things and often has a moralistic temper
(i.e., the way things *ought* to be done). The term is always used in
a descriptive (rather than prescriptive) sense in the NT and refers to human practices or actions, not to the products of a society.

Another Greek term that is similar in many ways to our English word *culture* is *paideia*. Derived from the Greek word for *child*, it refers to the training process of children and by extension, to their intellectual development. Thus *paideia* came to refer to culture in the sense of a body of learning or knowledge. (The other main use of *paideia* is *discipline* or *chastisement*. This is its primary use in the NT; e.g., Luke 23:16, 22; 1 Cor. 11:32; Heb. 12:5ff.) The use of *paideia* that is closest to the cultural sense of the term occurs in Acts 7:22 when Stephen says that Moses "was learned [*paideiuon*] in all the wisdom [*sophia*] of the Egyptians." By the standards of the royal Egyptian court, Moses was a *cultured* man. While *paideia* is a close equivalent to our word *culture*, it is different in that in some contexts it only refers to intellectual accomplishments.

There is no such correlate in the OT Hebrew. However it is most interesting to observe that the Hebrew word *abad*, usually rendered "work," "till/cultivate," "serve," or "worship" in English translations (see the extensive discussion of this term in part 1), shares a nearly identical range of meanings with the Latin *colere*, from which our word *culture* is derived (see discussion in the previous section of this introduction). The OT concept of work and our contemporary idea of culture are closely related. This only serves to amplify the importance that the early chapters of Genesis, and in particular Genesis 2:15, have concerning a biblical theology of culture. Mankind's call to *work* the ground is crucial to human self-understanding and self-purpose.

CULTURE AND THE COVENANT COMMUNITY

A quick scan of Church history will show that there has been a great deal of confusion on what the Christian response to existing culture should be. This is amply summarized in H. Richard Niebuhr's classic book *Christ and Culture*. Niebuhr's insightful analyses of historical positions on the issue is without parallel. He groups the major Christian responses to culture under the headings of "Christ against culture," "Christ of culture," "Christ above culture," "Christ and culture in paradox," and "Christ the transformer of culture." Thus he accounts for such divergent approaches to culture from those of the Anabaptists and the Church of Rome to the views of Tertullian, Augustine, and Luther.

Anyone interested in a Christian understanding of culture should read this book, even though it has strong neo-orthodox overtones (see the Recommended Reading List on page 123).

The heart of the confusion on this issue undoubtedly stems from the apparently conflicting perspectives on culture presented by the Old and New Testaments. I am fully convinced that there is no contradiction in the Scriptures on this issue (or on anything else for that matter); that the view of culture put forth in each testament makes perfect sense given the context in which they were written; and that taken as a whole, the Bible presents an unabashedly positive view of culture as a human undertaking.

The cultural perspective of the OT is one of *cultural transparency*. Although the nation of Israel was clearly aware of the surrounding pagan cultures, Israel was essentially a closed society and set out (with varying degrees of success) to develop obediently—according to the laws and precepts revealed through Moses and the prophets—the good land God had mercifully given to them. The Israelites did not set out self-consciously to make a *Hebrew* culture in contrast to the cultures of the other nations. Rather they focused on being faithful, in order to foster a culture which was fully in agreement with the teachings of Scripture. There clearly was a distinctively biblical Hebrew culture, although the OT covenant community did not spend much time ruminating on this fact as such.

The same is true of those Christian cultures which have been able by God's mercy to establish a full-blown society founded on scriptural principles. Here the cultural expression is Christian even if the members of that culture do not actively use the phrase "Christian culture." This fact is often lost on theologians, even those who should know better. For example, Reformed pastor Michael Horton in his book *Where in the World Is the Church?* asks, "Were great writers and artists of past centuries, like Milton, Bunyan, Handel, and Rembrandt, pioneers of 'Christian literature and art,' or were they simply Christians who created good art?" (p. 82). Horton then goes on to dismiss the notion of developing a specifically Christian aesthetic, literature, or musical form (pp. 32, 83ff). I would heartily agree with Dr. Horton that many believers who, for example, set out to write "Christian" novels end up with mediocre products which are (or should be) embarrassing to the Church. I would propose that the problem here is a truncated, shallow understanding of the term *Christian* and a fundamental ignorance of doctrine, which is rampant among today's evangelicals; the problem is not the use of the adjective as such. These so-called "Christian" novels are in reality *sub-*Christian.

C. S. Lewis framed the problem this way:

> The word *religion* is extremely rare in the NT or the writings of the mystics. The reason is simple. Those attitudes and practices to which we give the collective name *religion* are themselves concerned with religion hardly at all. To be religious is to have one's attention fixed on God and one's neighbor in relation to God. Therefore, almost by definition, a religious man, or a man when he is being religious, is not thinking about religion; he hasn't the time. (emphasis original)

If Rembrandt would have been puzzled by the question of whether or not he was a Christian artist (p. 86), it would have only been because he was not (presumably) accustomed to thinking in these terms. (Lewis might say that he was too busy with his art to dwell self-consciously on his Christian faith.) Faithful artists in Calvinistic Holland took their biblical worldview (but not their salvation!) for granted; thinking and working in biblical terms was simply who they were. There was no pagan or secularistic opposition to their faith that stirred them to think in terms of Christian versus non-Christian culture. (If anything, Reformed artists would have thought in terms of being Protestant artists rather than Romish during Rembrandt's epoch. A point to ponder: Did their failure to see their culture in self-consciously Christian terms contribute to the Dutch society's fall from grace by the nineteenth century?)

It was exactly this sort of ideological, pagan opposition to the faith—in the form of Hellenism—that formed the cultural backdrop of the NT. Thus the dominant cultural perspective of the NT is one of *cultural antithesis*. It is within this context that the apostles urged believers to avoid the world (e.g., James 4:4; 1 Jn 2:15f) and warned that the things of this world could be a dangerous distraction (Matt. 13:22; Luke 18:22). At first reading, these passages seem to teach that believers should withdraw from cultural endeavors as much as possible. An emphasis on these Scripture texts has led to the ascetic tradition within Christianity; this is embodied in many monastic orders and in the Anabaptist movement. But taking the whole of the NT into the mix, we see that the term *world* cannot in these negative passages refer to the physical earth (1 Cor. 5:10); rather it refers to the whole sinful social order that is in systematic rebellion against God. The apostles urged Christians not to be conformed to the common beliefs and values of a pagan society but, rather, to have the totality of their thoughts shaped by the doctrines of Scripture alone (Rom. 12:2). The NT emphatically teaches that the physical things of this world are good and to be enjoyed within the bounds of God's law (Luke 7:34; John 2:10; 1 Cor. 10:3; Col. 2:20ff; 1 Tim. 4:3–4). The NT writers did not oppose the OT desire to found a culture based on scriptural principles. They recognized that Christians, faced with a hostile, blatantly anti-Christian society, must remove themselves from the harmful effects of that society as much as possible, especially when political and social circumstances make the forming of a biblical society on a national scale impractical. When faced with such a prospect, Christian culture must begin on a small scale as a faithful counter-culture (Matt. 5:14–16; Zech. 4:10).

Niebuhr's book primarily deals with the Christian response to existing cultures rather than culture-making as a particular relationship with the earth. While the issue of the covenant community's response to the culture they live in is of critical practical importance, it misses an important point. (Most evangelicals have correctly agreed with Niebuhr's "Christ the transformer of culture" position and have focused their cultural efforts on working with existing cultural forms, co-opting or reworking them, with mixed results.) The primary focus of our cultural efforts must be our call to *transform the earth*, not to transform the existing culture, although this, when performed according to biblical principles, is a lawful, worthwhile activity. We would also do well to avoid the prevailing "culture war" view: culture seen as an ideological/religious struggle between good and evil, godly and rebellious art, literature, politics, philosophy, etc. While we must never lose sight of the *antithesis* and Paul's call for us to "take every thought captive to the obedience of Christ" (2 Cor. 10:4–5), we must assert that culture is, at its foundation, about *building* and not about *conflict*. Doing culture from a positive, earth-transformational perspective will help us build a more comprehensive, radical, holistic culture in line with the principles of Scripture, and it will provide us with less opportunity to compromise with the anti-biblical values and beliefs embedded in the pagan, unbelieving cultures we might encounter.

TOWARD A BIBLICAL THEOLOGY OF CULTURE

Geerhardus Vos in *Biblical Theology* observes that one of the key components of the discipline of biblical theology is that it seeks to study God's character, purposes, actions, and revelation *within history*—as they have been unfolded in time:

> [Biblical Theology] differs from Systematic Theology, not in being more Biblical, or adhering more closely to the truths of the Scriptures, but in that its principle of organizing the Biblical material is historical rather than logical. . . . Biblical Theology deals with the material from the historical standpoint, seeking to exhibit the organic growth or development of the truths of Special Revelation from the primitive pre-redemptive Special Revelation given in Eden to the close of the NT canon." (p. v–vi)

This book sets out to be a biblical theology of culture. Beginning with God's commands to Adam and Eve in the first two chapters of Genesis and ending with the disclosure of the New Jerusalem in the closing chapters of Revelation, this book examines culture within its redemptive-historical context. In fact, I have found it helpful to see culture operating within two broad strands of history which are decreed and ruled by God: *culturative* history (the history of the process of culture) and *redemptive* history (the history of human salvation wrought by God). I should stress at the outset that these two strands of history are not unconnected from one another, but since the Fall, they have been closely intertwined and in some instances (i.e., the building of the tabernacle and the Temple) have been identical. Nevertheless these two historical strands must be considered separately for at least two reasons. First, man's "cultural mandate"—the call to rule, fill, and transform the earth—was established before the Fall and exists independently of man's need for redemption. God clearly had an initial, basic plan for the development of the newly created earth, which included mankind's cultural involvement. Since this plan was instituted prior to the fall of man into sin, we may properly call culture (along with the other "pre-redemptive" institutions of marriage and worship) *normative* for mankind. Second, it becomes clear both in the pages of Scripture and by historical observation (for example the *Byōdō-in* temple discussed at the opening of this introduction) that it has pleased God to allow a significant portion of the cultural development of the earth to be effectuated by those outside the covenant. Although the better of these works are destined by God to be taken away from unbelievers and given to the elect for their godly use, nevertheless it seems best to say that these cultural efforts stand outside of (separate from) redemptive history. Part 1 of this book, "A Positive Theology of Culture," outlines the basic scriptural teachings on God's plan and purpose for culture; it relies primarily on the early chapters of Genesis.

Of course things changed very soon after the cultural mandate was proclaimed by God. The Fall introduced the need for redemption and a Redeemer in order for mankind to continue in a state of fellowship (rather than wrath) with God. From the "mother promise" of Genesis 3:15 to the establishment of a renewed people on the New Earth in the eternal presence of God and the Lamb who was slain, we see the divine initiative to save mankind unfurled in redemptive history. Here we see God not merely restoring mankind to a holy state of worship and fellowship through the shed blood of Jesus Christ but also restoring mankind that he might fulfill with perfection the original cultural mandate. This relationship between culture and God's redemptive acts, and culture's place within the restoration of the earth is outlined in part 2, "Culture and Redemption."

In a brief concluding postscript, "Culture and the Sabbath," I try to demonstrate how the sabbath is a holy day of worship and feasting and an emblem of the eternal rest from sin and toil we will enjoy on the New Earth; the sabbath was instituted by God as a constant reminder of the goodness of creation and work (Ex. 20:11) and of man's need for liberation from his slavery to sin and misery in this present fallen world (Deut. 5:15). The sabbath serves as a vital means of contrast between man's calling to work (*culture*) and man's calling to worship (*cultus*). Even in this distinction of days, we see that, ideally, our work is to be done in a worshipful manner and that our worship is enhanced by cultural products. I propose that this twofold distinction was not present before the Fall: man's cultural work was to be perfect, utterly transparent worship directed to the Creator. At the Fall, this transparency was broken. But it will be restored again when we are ushered into the glorious New Jerusalem, to serve God once again in Paradise—perfectly free from sin and toil—as kings and priests and culture-makers, to the everlasting glory of God.

The basic points I observe about culture are summarized in ten propositions. These are explored in parts 1 and 2 of this book. I have tried to bolster my arguments with numerous biblical texts, many of which have been printed out in full. I implore you to read this book with your Bible open, to examine these texts in their context (as well as the others that are only cited) to see if they do in fact say what I propose about man's cultural mandate (Acts 17:11). It is my prayer that this book will help the bride of Jesus Christ recover her vital call to rule, fill, work, and preserve the earth as a high and indispensable priority. Culture-making is not optional; it is a command which from the very beginning has never been revoked. May we—by God's grace!—be allowed to build a culture worthy of our Redeemer's precious Name.

PART ONE:

A POSITIVE THEOLOGY
OF CULTURE

The opening pages of the Bible provide us with a normative picture of creation and mankind. Sin was not yet on the scene. All that existed in the newly formed, beautiful creation was good and in perfect harmony and peace (*shalom*) with the Almighty Creator. It is in the midst of this sinless world that God gave mankind the cultural mandate. Before sin and salvation were even issues, man was commanded to rule and fill the earth, and work (till) and keep (guard) the splendid garden which was his home. In these four tasks—ruling, filling, working, and keeping—we see culture in seed form. Human beings were called to transform the original garden into a beautiful city, which is the eventual goal of human history as revealed in the final pages of the Bible. This comprehensive transformation was possible only when human beings formed communities where a wide diversity of talents and skills could be developed and pooled together in order to complete the monumental cultural task—to the glory of God!

A positive theology of culture is stated in the six propositions which follow.

1.

There are two principal strands of human history: culturative history and redemptive history.

Man is neither angel nor brute, and the unfortunate thing is that he who would act the angel acts the brute.

—Pascal, *Pensées*

"What is man?" This is a question which has vexed human philosophers—amateur and professional, Christian and non-Christian—throughout the centuries. There is no easy answer; at least, there is no easy *comprehensive* answer. Pascal in his *Pensées* found that it was easier to state what man is not (see quote above). While sharing eternity with the angels (Eccl. 3:11) and flesh and blood with the beasts, man is ultimately something quite distinct from either. This readily agrees with the worldview of David, the royal psalmist who sang:

> What is man that You are mindful of him,
> And the son of man that You visit him?
> For You have made him a little lower than the angels
> And You have crowned him with glory and honor. (Ps. 8:4–5)

The Bible here and elsewhere declares that man is a creature of a peculiar glory and honor, holding a place just below the heavenly creatures in the overall scheme of things. In the sight of God, he is of immense value. Man is a mere creature who holds dominion over the rest of the physical creation, including the animals:

A Note on Terminology

Throughout this book the term *culturative* is used to denote mankind's culture-making activities. Clearly the standard adjectival form of the word culture—cultural—could have been used. But there is considerable ambiguity in how this word is commonly employed. For example, "cultural history" might refer to the strand of human history concerned with culture-making, but it could just as well be understood as human history taken from an anthropological perspective (akin to the field of study called "material culture"), as compared to socio-history or intellectual history. I have chosen to use the new word *culturative* to focus exclusively on *the process* of culture-making—those activities associated with mankind's rule over creation. Hence "culturative history" refers to the history of the process of human communities transforming the earth from its natural beginning to a developed and improved state, ever more productive and beautiful than the original.

You have made him to have dominion
over the work of your hands;
You have put all things under his feet,
All sheep and oxen—
Even the beasts of the field,
The birds of the air,
And the fish of the sea
That pass through the paths of the sea.
(Ps. 8:6–8; cf. Gen. 1:26–27)

This takes us immediately back to the opening chapter of Genesis, where we learn that man—male and female—is made in the "image" and "likeness" of God; he reflects in some marvelous way key aspects of the divine character. Theologians have concluded that the *imago dei* includes (but is not limited to) man's intellectual faculties: his ability to make moral choices, his capacity for self-reflection and self-criticism, his propensity for social relationships, and above all, his (apparently) unique role within all of physical creation to appreciate and enjoy God's majestic character and to respond back to Him in self-conscious praise.

All of these remarkable capabilities and attributes ultimately depend on another property which man shares with the rest of God's creation: *existence*. Man and everything else to be found in God's glorious creation are not some dream coursing through the mind of God. Creation is real. Men and women exist in a particular time and place which God has appointed beforehand for them to occupy (Acts 17:26). As such, they are a part of *history*.

Two of the most notable strands of human history will be discussed in this book. One strand—*redemptive* history—has rightly occupied the central focus of the Church for as long as it has had a historical consciousness. The Bible is the book where we read about the dramatic events which form the prominent milestones along the highway of salvation history: the Fall, the gracious covenants with Noah and Abraham, the spectacular exodus, the splendid reign of Solomon in the Land of Promise, and eventually, the return of the King of kings and the consummation of all things. The most thrilling aspect of all is that redemptive history involves nothing less than the victorious death and resurrection of the incarnate God-Man Jesus Christ to save a peculiar people for Himself. This is arguably the hinge upon which all of history—human and cosmic—turns.

Nevertheless, this is not the whole story. Before concepts such as sin, death, alienation, redemption, restoration, etc., were ever on the historical scene, there was another more basic strand of human history—*culturative* history. As we will examine shortly, man was given the task to order, develop, and embellish God's splendid creation, to realize the multifarious potentialities which were embedded within it. All of this was commanded before the fall of man into sin. All of this was an integral part of God's "very good" creation order (Gen. 1:31). Christians, in their zeal to honor God for His abundant redemptive graces and to proclaim this salvation to the whole of creation, have all but lost a strong sense of man's original cultural calling. In far too many cases, a vision for man's vital role as a culture-maker is altogether absent from the believer's mind. The primary goal of this book is to help the Church recover a biblical vision for culture-making; culture has a central place in God's overall purpose for the human race.

While on the subject of human history, it is worth making a few observations about the nature of history before exploring the specifics of culturative history and its relationship to redemptive history. The first thing to observe about history is that it is ruled by our Sovereign Father. All that happens in creation—from the fall of a tiny sparrow in some forgotten forest to the lumps of iron ore which were mined, smelted, forged, and eventually hammered through the hands and feet of the Lamb of God—comes not by chance but from the loving hand of a caring God. Horrible things may and do happen, but we have the assurance that God is in complete control, and all things—appearances not withstanding—are being directed together for the ultimate good of God's people and to His everlasting praise (Rom. 8:28; 11:33–36). Hence we may be assured that our prayers are not in vain. We may observe that God does not merely direct the timing and sequence of historical events, but He is also continually upholding and preserving each and every creature within creation so that the events can even occur! (Heb. 1:3; Col. 1:17).

Against the backdrop of our Father's providential rule of time and place, we may assert another amazing truth: man the *image bearer* is somehow involved in the shaping of the history that God ultimately controls. We are bestowed with a will. We make real choices which have real historical consequences. Sometimes our choices are the result of careful, thoughtful planning; at other times, we decide on whim. Yet God uses all of our decisions—great and small—to affect the course of historical events. At first glance it seems impossible that the puny actions of mortal man (a mere puppet?) have any real significance in the face of the Almighty's determinative, unstoppable decree. "Who has resisted His will?" (Rom. 9:19), one might well ask. Yet the historical choices of men and women do matter because God has decreed it so! The Westminster divines put it this way: "God from all eternity did . . . freely and unchangeably ordain whatsoever comes to pass, yet so as thereby neither . . . is the liberty or contingency of second causes taken away, but rather established" (WCF chap. 3.1; cf. WCF chap. 4.2). We may safely conclude both that the God of Abraham, Isaac, and Jacob is the Lord of history and that this Great God is pleased to give man a significant, even necessary, place in His history. Man is not merely to be acted upon by the Creator; he is to be a kind of actor-collaborator within the Playwright's grand scheme.

2.

Culturative history is God's unfolding purpose for man, in which mankind plays a chief role in the development and transformation of the earth from garden-paradise to the glorious city of God.

Genesis 1:26 teaches us that God had a purpose in creating man in His image: namely, that man should have dominion over all living creatures and that he should multiply and spread out over the world, subduing it. If now we comprehend the force of this subduing under the term culture, *now generally used for it, we can say that* culture *in its broadest sense is the purpose for which God created man after His image."*

—Herman Bavinck, *Our Reasonable Faith*

The Bible begins in a garden and ends in a city. This basic fact of biblical history is obvious, but it is often overlooked because of the emphasis on redemptive history and the life and work of Jesus Christ. But in order to get a handle on why man was created and placed on the earth, this fact and its implications must be fully understood. Human history from the very outset has had a decided direction and purpose. This basic, historical movement is diagramed in figure 1:

Figure 1: The culturative direction of history before the fall

Splendid Garden   ⟶   Glorious City (Goal)
culturative progress over time

Paradise: a Link between the Past and the Future

"Paradise" is taken from the ancient Persian for an enclosed or walled garden or park used by Oriental kings and nobles. These parks were often quite large, included extensive tree plantings and man-made irrigation channels, and were stocked with wild animals to be hunted as a part of the leisure activities of the court. The word *paradise* was a loan word used in both Hebrew and Greek and is found in both the OT and NT. The first uses of the term in the OT were during the time of Solomon (Eccl. 2:5; Song. 4:13), who undoubtedly learned of the term from his many foreign visitors. OT use of the word is confined to actual gardens or parks (cf. Neh. 2:8). However, in extra-biblical Hebrew writings, there is mention of a "concealed paradise," which is the place

Human history begins in a garden located in a place called "Eden" (Gen. 2:8). The term *eden* seems to refer to a specific geographic locale. While the Hebrew word *eden* might have been derived from the Akkadian/Sumerian *edinu/edin*, meaning *a plain or steppe*, it is more likely a play on the Hebrew *adan*, which carries with it the idea of luxury, finery, or delicacy (cf. Ps. 36:8). It was in accordance with this understanding of the term that the translators of the Septuagint and the Vulgate translated *eden* as "pleasure." In later OT uses of the term (e.g., Is. 51:3; Ezek. 36:35; Joel 2:3), *eden* is described as a place of fertile abundance as a result of the LORD's blessing and is usually contrasted to the desert wilderness. The picture of the original Garden of Eden is one of complete happiness: fruitfulness, glory, and beauty—a fitting reflection of the Creator's own superabundant splendor.

There are many striking similarities between the Garden of Eden described in the beginning of Genesis 2 and the New Jerusalem which appears at the end of history (Rev. 21–22). In both we find a river which is located near the tree of life. God is present in the midst of both the garden and the city, and most heartening of all, mankind is there, too, enjoying unrestricted fellowship with his Creator. We must note the differences as well. The two great "lamps" which ruled over the garden (Gen. 1:16) seem to be nowhere in sight in the city. God and the Lamb are in their place, bathing the city with their glorious light. But there are other remarkable additions as well: walls, gates, and streets. Where did these come from?

The Garden of Eden was apparently devoid of architectural structures (with the possible exception of a wall—the Hebrew term for garden implies a place that is "protected," presumably by a wall or hedge). What the garden did have was a vast array of beautiful fruit-bearing trees and other vegetation and animal life of every size and description. Over all this man was to rule. He was not merely to enjoy all that God had made, but he was to work it and keep it. This implied that from the very beginning mankind was expected to bring changes to the creation, that some sort of transformation was to take place. And these changes were not to be only a rearrangement or reorganization of the plants and animal life in the garden. Artificial things (i.e., things made by *artifice*=human skill) were to be added to the mix. That non-"natural" additions to the original creation are divinely sanctioned is boldly affirmed by the arrival of the heavenly city. Walls, gates, and streets are not an evil intrusion into the natural ideal but are all part of God's plan, which will be finally brought into full completion at the consummation.

Mankind was given the privilege of actually improving upon the original, natural creation. One only has to contemplate the amazing variety of roses—their size, color,

where the souls of the patriarchs and other righteous persons are gathered after death (cf. Luke 16:22).

This would seem to be what Jesus had in mind when He said to the thief on the cross, "Today you will be with me in Paradise" (Luke 23:43). Paul also used the term to describe heaven (or some other non-earthly place) in 2 Corinthians 12:4. The use of the word *paradise* comes into strong eschatological focus in Revelation 2:7: "To him who overcomes I will give to eat from the tree of life, which is in the midst of the Paradise of God." This is a clear reference to what is described at the end of Revelation, where the New Jerusalem has the "tree of life . . . the leaves [of which] were for the healing of the nations" (Rev. 22:2-3). John's choice of words appears to be even more striking when we note that *paradise* was used in the Septuagint for the Garden of Eden. This emphasizes the thematic unity of Genesis 2 and Revelation 21-22. There is a profound thread which moves though the course of the entire Bible, from the original garden to the heavenly Jerusalem. The latter place is described both as a garden [*paradeisos*] and a city [*polis*], making it the paradigmatic garden-city.

shape, and fragrance—developed from an ordinary wild ancestor, or hybrid vegetables, which have much higher yields than their natural counterparts while at the same time having higher pest resistance, to see that betterment is possible. But the development of creation is made possible only by God. It is God who vested the earth with a rich array of potentialities to be discovered and used in order to bring improvement upon nature. It is God who placed His image upon mankind and gave him the desire and the abilities to bring out the possibilities hidden within that creation. Thus, all of the glory for the culturative development of the earth belongs to our Father, who sovereignly rules over the culturative process. To ascribe glory to ourselves in any way is the rank idolatry of humanism (see Dan. 4:28–36).

A number of years ago in New York City, I spoke at a symposium on architecture and Christianity. During a question-and-answer session, I found myself in a somewhat heated discussion with one of the members of the audience (a practicing architect!) over which biblical paradigm—the garden or the city—was ultimate. He proposed that architecture was a kind of necessary evil: if sin had never entered the world, we would still be in a garden paradise devoid of built structures. I argued in favor of the city as the ultimate goal towards which human progress should strive. As our discussion began to come to a boil, a clever pastor in the audience rose up and yelled, "You are both wrong! What God has in mind is a garden-city!" (Since this was the name of a nearby Long Island suburb, we all broke out in laughter.) This pastor was absolutely right. The trees in the heavenly city (Rev. 22:2) point to the fact that the garden was not left behind entirely. God's intent is that nature, man-made structures, and well crafted artifacts be married together into a glorious, harmonious whole.

It is important for us to recapture the biblical vision of the garden-city—a global network of cities, parklands, agricultural fields and groves, forests and wilderness preserves—as the goal of mankind's culturative activities. The garden-city points to the necessity of a well-developed community to achieve culturative success. The glory of the heavenly Jerusalem implies that the culturative development of the earth will have a considerable richness and scope. This will only be possible as significant numbers of people, blessed with diverse gifts and skills, live and work together toward a common, God-defined end. Where do men and women live together in significant numbers so that this noble end may be reached? The city! The city is both the means and the goal of our culturative calling before God. The garden is only the starting point. The garden-city also implies that there is to be harmony between humans and nature, that the works of man and the works of nature are both vital and are both to co-exist and complement one another.

As we look at the architecture of the New Jerusalem, it is not altogether dissimilar to the buildings and structures we have encountered in our present world. Surely the materials are far more exquisite than those of the finest palace ever built, and the workmanship is impeccable, yet the walls and gates and streets were easily recognized by the apostle. But for their unspeakable beauty, we might be tempted to wonder if they are the result of human efforts like the parapets, portals, and boulevards we see in this present world. Could this be the case? At first glance Scripture seems to teach otherwise. Hebrews 11:10 tells us that Abraham was waiting for the city "whose builder and maker was God," an obvious allusion to the city of Revelation 21–22. This would seem to settle the question of the city's origin. But it should be noted that in other places the Bible alludes to works and actions of God which are actually carried out by human agency (e.g., Acts 1:1).

3.

Culture is the concretization—the rendering in some permanent form—of mankind's culturative acts, commonly manifested in man-made objects, structures, texts, etc. Such artifacts stand apart from but (ideally) work in harmony with God's natural creation or "nature."

> *Art, like morality, consists in*
> *drawing the line somewhere.*
>
> —G.K. Chesterton

As man sets out to fulfill his calling to transform the earth from its original natural state into a glorious garden-city, it is clear that he must *do* something. It is not enough simply to think about the changes that could be made. Real action must be taken. From the very beginning, Adam responded to the creative acts of the LORD with culturative acts of his own. First, he undertook the task of naming the animals (Gen. 2:19–20), which involved careful observation and analysis—the basis of all science. Shortly thereafter, Adam composed a brief poem extolling the virtues of his perfect companion, the woman (Gen. 2:23). Here we see the beginning of the arts. These two pre-redemptive acts did not yet bring any alteration to the natural landscape, but it was soon to come.

Man was assigned an even more basic culturative act—

growing crops (Gen. 2:5, 15)—which involved at its inception cutting open the ground to plant seed. There can be no harvest without plowing, and plowing alters the virgin landscape forever. Thus a real concrete change had to take place. Likewise, buildings are to be built and artifacts are to be manufactured and placed within the landscape as part of the culturative transformation of the earth. These man-made structures and objects (along with texts) must not merely be brought into *existence;* in order for the garden-city to be established finally, some of them must *endure.* Artifacts which perish over time and are forgotten, even though they may have contributed greatly to the civilization which made and used them, can have no impact on subsequent culturative processes and thus will have no place in the vast mosaic of human works which furnish the finished garden-city (see discussion at the end of part 2).

The artifacts human beings place into the landscape will be distinct from nature. Man is not the only creature who builds structures, fashions objects, or emits purposeful sounds. The animal world is full of fascinating examples of such activities. (One of my favorite Library of Congress subject headings is "Animals as Architects.") But, with the possible exception of select large primates, animals do these activities strictly by instinct. Beavers only build dams and lodges; they never experiment with other structures. Spiders (Charlotte not withstanding!) never deviate from prescribed patterns of web-making; in fact, their methods are so uniform that experts can often determine from a particular web which species made it. Even chimpanzees who seem to be able to master rudimentary sign language can take this talent only so far. They do not (at least not yet) create poetry or put on plays. (Both of these *human* activities involve the sophisticated manipulation of symbols which are beyond the animal world.) Similarly, chimps enjoy experimenting with paints, and though they show an affinity for color and balanced compositions, they never reach the point of copying or symbolically representing the things they encounter in the world. Because animals act and create within the bounds set for them by their Maker (we are tempted to say that they are "programmed" to perform the activities they do), we see their artifacts as being "natural" or a part of *nature.*

Man, because he is made in the "image" and "likeness" of God, is endowed with many extraordinary attributes which enable him to rise above the recurring, rhythmical processes of nature to impose his ideas and designs upon the original, "untouched" landscape. Undoubtedly, man's unique *historical consciousness* sets him apart from the animals and contributes to our ability to make culture which stands apart from nature. Men and women have the capacity to perceive and reflect on what has gone on in the past, to choose to imitate what has been done before, or to deliberately strike out into new creative territory. We have the ability to think in terms of the future, to mull over various potential alternatives, and to devise and execute remarkably complex projects that profoundly impact our environment. Because of our historical consciousness, we have the potential to pass on our tastes and insights to others (usually through the family) and to build upon and embellish what has already been achieved. Thus we may speak of cultural progress, growth, and maturation. Animals, on the other hand, will continue to undertake the same range of activities century after century with no behavioral change. We may summarize these differences by saying that animals are *reactive* toward their environment, whereas humans may be *proactive*.

Man also has a unique *moral capacity*. Unlike the rest of nature, we have the ability to choose self-consciously to act in a way contrary to the way God intends for us to act. We call this sin. This has led to disastrous consequences. Instead of being true to our original calling to work and keep the earth, enhancing its fruitfulness to the glory of the Creator, we have chosen to exploit the earth's bounty by neglecting the balance between development *and* preservation or we have set out deliberately to hurt and destroy God's good creation for nothing more than the perverse "thrill" of it. Man's moral capacity also colors his cultural activities. Our artifacts, texts, and structures all have profound expressive potential, which mirror the personality of the individuals or communities which make them, as well as embodying the moral orientation—good or evil—of their makers. Thankfully, mankind does not only have the ability to fall into sin but also the potential to be redeemed. God restores us to a state where we can do good (indeed, eventually to a state in which good is *all* we will do!) and carry out our culturative calling with joyful obedience.

Ideally, mankind's culturative transformation of the earth should work in harmony with God's original creation order. The goal (as was alluded to earlier in this study) is to create a garden-city, where the beauty of man-made works and the glory of nature are wed in a mutually-enhancing whole. The vast potential for culture-nature synergism was first brought to my attention several years ago by a Christian sculptor who shared with me the breathtaking experience of seeing the Golden Gate Bridge for the first time. Anyone who has been there cannot help being captivated by the sheer grandeur of the natural site: the rolling golden hills spilling down to meet the vast, open ocean expanse. Against this dramatic backdrop is the bridge, reaching across the water in a graceful sweep of arcs subtly punctuated by the two slender towers. Even the bridge's color enhances the sense of mutuality. So powerful is this marriage of seascape and steel that it becomes almost impossible, having experienced it, to conceive of the place without the bridge. Undoubtedly the opening to San Francisco Bay was beautiful in its own right before the introduction of the bridge. And the bridge, if placed in another, less spectacular site, would still be a classic. But, in bringing the two together, we are privileged to experience both in a new light, to see the innate beauty of each in a fresh, exciting way which would have eluded us if the bridge had never been built there. The Golden Gate Bridge and other remarkable examples of nature-culture collaboration (e.g., Frank Lloyd Wright's *Fallingwater*; the Temple complex perched majestically upon Mount Zion—Ps. 48:2) should be held up as examples of how our artifacts ought to work in harmony with nature, not destroying but enhancing God's good creation.

4.

Culture is an essential outworking of mankind's unique place within God's creation as image-bearer of God. Man's cultural activities grow out of his special relationship to the earth (*adam/ adamah*) to work and keep it. Man is commanded to utilize his innate skills to develop the potentialities "hidden" in the earth waiting to be discovered and realized.

> *We are not worthy to enjoy the condition of our first father, who was to live in a pleasant setting without having to work hard. Nevertheless, before sin entered the world, and before we were condemned by God to painful and difficult work, it was necessary for men to occupy themselves with some work. Why? Because it was against our nature for us to be useless blocks of wood.*
>
> —John Calvin, *Sermons on Deuteronomy*

As far as we know from the Scriptures, man is the only creature that was made in God's image (Gen. 1:26; 9:6). We may further assert that the *imago dei* is inextricably linked with man's role as culture-maker. Only man has ability to move beyond the uniform rhythms of nature and transform the earth according to his own imaginative devices. It would appear likely, then, that

Mankind's Marriage to the Earth

The entire book of Genesis is full of word play and puns, many of which are rich with meaning and irony. We will now focus on two such puns found in Genesis 2: the play of the man (adam) coming from and working the ground (adamah) in verses 5, 7, and 15; and the play of the words man (ish) and woman (ishshah) in the inaugural poem of v. 23. One of the linguistic ironies of the Hebrew language is found in the couplet man/ground. Even though the man was taken from the dust of the ground in history, etymologically, adamah is taken from its root, adam. We can infer from this that the ground (and, correspondingly, the earth) was made for and in terms of the man and not vice versa, at least conceptually.

While there is a vital linguistic link between the words for man and ground, the ish/ishshah couplet is only a pun (ish is actually spelled "iysh," but the Yod is silent; ishshah is a root word in the Hebrew). Nevertheless the superficial similarities between the two word

man's unique gift for culture flows out of his unique creaturely character. We have already examined two principle outworkings of this image which have important ramifications for culture-making: our distinctive historical consciousness and our moral awareness. We shall now briefly look at the four main tasks God assigned to the human race at the beginning of creation and observe how they relate to the culturative process.

In virtually the same breath that God announces His intention "to make man in Our image, according to Our likeness" (Gen. 1:26), He charges the man and woman to "be fruitful and multiply, *fill* the earth and *subdue* it, have dominion over the fish of the sea, over the birds of the air, and over every living thing that moves on the earth" (Gen. 1:28). This verse is often referred to as the "cultural mandate" with good reason. Mankind is to fill the earth and to subdue it. The first task, "filling," is to be carried out by the fruitfulness of married couples (the man and the woman in v. 27 are presented as the normative family unit; cf. Gen. 2:24). Here we can see the *scope* of the culturative enterprise. Through the act of "multiplying," the human race was to accomplish the gradual filling of the entire earth, not just a tiny portion of it (i.e., the garden). Men and women were to beget, raise, and then send out culture-makers into every corner of God's creation.

The text also explicitly says that we are to "rule" over the earth as kings (cf. 1 Pet. 2:9; Rev. 1:6; 5:10; 22:5) by "subduing" the land and having "dominion" over the animals who inhabited the creation

(Ps. 8:6–8; Gen. 9:2). This is the *goal* of the culturative enterprise. We rule as vice-regents of the Creator, bringing the whole earth under human subjection so that we in turn may present the creation to God. Our rule of the earth has its ultimate fulfillment in Christ's perfect rule (1 Cor. 15:24–28; Heb. 2:6–9). Just as a king has the right to impose his will upon the people he rules (which is a *good* thing when done according to the precepts of God; cf. Ps. 72), so man was given the imperative to shape God's creation in line with his good desires (which before the Fall were completely devoid of evil—Gen 1:31). It is important to emphasize that our rule (along with all other creaturely authority) is derived from and strictly regulated by the King (Rom. 13:1–2). Thus our cultural dominion is to be exercised in terms of our subjection to God's authority over us as His creatures. As we seek to put our "mark" on the creation, we must do so only as we ourselves are being shaped by God's law. Any failure on the part of man to follow God's directives will result in the horrible oppression and destruction of the original fruitful creation (Rom. 8:19ff; Rev. 11:18).

The third and fourth tasks are found in Genesis 2:15: "Then the LORD God took the man and put him in the Garden of Eden to *tend* and *keep* it." These two complementary activities summarize the two *modes* of the culturative enterprise. First, man is called to "tend" (NKJV) or "work" (NIV) the garden. (Given that the human race was to spread out and rule over the entire earth [Gen. 1:28], it seems fair to conclude that what is true about working the ground in

pairs are worth noting. The essential difference between each pair of words is an added *He* ("h") at the end of one of the word pairs. A conceptual analogy may be drawn between each pair:

adam
———
adamah

as

ish
———
ishshah

Just as the *ish* is the husband of the *ishshah,* so the man (*ha-adam*) is the husband of the ground (*adamah*). As a husband is expected to lovingly provide for his bride, cherishing and nourishing her (Eph. 5:29) and thereby enhancing her health and beauty, so the man was to work and keep the ground/earth, enhancing its fruitfulness. Likewise, just as a husband will gain children only if he "interacts" with his wife, so the earth will yield its fruit only through culturative interaction. The English language ironically captures this idea with the word *husbandry.*

Marriage is a fitting analogy to describe

man's culturative relationship with the earth. Just as a marriage provides the appropriate lawful setting for the expression of human sexuality, so mankind must seek to exercise his culture-making activities within the bounds defined by the Creator. We must avoid the pitfall of culturative *celibacy*, altogether removing ourselves from the development of the earth, as many contemporary environmentalists would propose. And we must avoid the culturative *rape* of nature, going beyond the limits of our original calling both to *preserve* and to *develop* the earth's hidden potential and fruitfulness.

Genesis 2 was to apply ultimately to the earth as a whole; the global perspective of Genesis 1 and the Edenic perspective of Genesis 2 are different takes on the same cultural reality.) The Hebrew word rendered "tend" or "work" is *abad*, which has a fairly wide range of meanings centered around the idea of work. The term seems to be derived from Aramaic and/or Arabic roots meaning *to make* or *to worship* a deity. A closely related Hebrew term is *ebed*, meaning *slave*, that is, someone who works for another. Depending on its context, *abad* can be rendered "to work" (often modified to fit the setting, e.g., "tilling" the ground; cf. Gen. 4:2; Deut. 21:4; Ex. 35:24; 1 Chr. 4:21), "to serve" (when used in relationship to a person, usually as a slave; Gen. 29:15; Ex. 1:14), or "to worship" (i.e., to work for God within the cultic context—Num. 3:7f; Deut. 4:19). Contrary to many recent renderings of Genesis 2:15 by Christian environmentalists, the context does not allow *abad* to be translated as "serve" (i.e., "to *serve* . . . it [the garden]"); Hebrew usage reserves this meaning of *abad* only when the action is directed toward a person. Such a rendering makes no sense in light of mankind's worldwide rule outlined in the first chapter of Genesis.

The idea of *work* is a major theme in the early chapters of Genesis (compare the use of *abad* in Genesis 2:15 with Genesis 2:5, 3:23, 4:2, and 4:12; the text of these verses are listed on p. 47). The fact that a generic term for work is used in Genesis 2:15 brings the universality of the command into focus. Clearly the most all-embracing idea of culturative transformation is in view. The cultivation of the garden is not a passive activity. It involves a definite interaction with and alteration of the original landscape. We might say that man was required to "get his hands dirty" in fulfilling this aspect of his calling.

Man is called to "work" the earth in order to uncover the rich potentialities "hidden," as it were, beneath the earth's surface. On the most basic, agri*cultural* level, man cuts into the earth and sows seed, which grows up into plants, which, when carefully tended, yield fruit in their appointed seasons. Dig deeper and the earth will yield still more riches: precious stones and gold (Gen. 2:11–12; Job 28); ore which can be smelted to make metals; and basic chemical raw materials which can be synthesized into pigments and dyes for art works, fertilizers to increase crop yields, or rocket fuel to explore God's vast universe. Other parts of the creation can be transformed as well: wood can be fashioned into flutes for the praise of God or timbers for buildings; stones can be dressed and fitted into walls, etc.

The answer to the opening question of the Westminster Shorter Catechism states: "Man's chief end is to glorify God and to enjoy him forever." How does glorifying and enjoying God square with man's calling to "work" the Garden to transform it into a global garden-city? Part of this answer is revealed in the multiple meanings of *abad,* the Hebrew term for work discussed earlier. As human beings *worked* the land, they were simultaneously *serving* their Lord and *worshiping* their Creator. Man, in his original state of innocence, performed all his activities to the glory of God. Work, human relationships, communication with God, etc., were all transparently undertaken as self-conscious service to the Lord. Likewise, when the first man and woman gazed upon the beauty of the garden and were moved by the vastness of the nighttime sky, they were not merely enjoying their natural surroundings but were appreciating and reveling in God's creative character (Ps. 19). As mankind came to understand the wisdom and order of God's good creation, he would have performed his culturative activities in response to and as a reflection of God's creative acts. Making and praising (*ora et labora*) were one and the same before the Fall.

In addition to his calling to "work" the garden, man is commanded to "keep" it. The Hebrew word here is *shamar,* which means *to exercise great care over*. In the context of Genesis 2:15, the term carries with it the idea of *taking care of* or *guarding* something of value either from damage or from an outside intruder or enemy (cf. Gen. 3:24; 4:9; 30:31; 2 Sam. 15:16). The same term is traditionally translated as "keep" in the Aaronic benediction (Num. 6:24), denoting the way in which God tenderly guards us and preserves our lives before His face. While the term may point to how Adam was called to guard the garden from evil intruders (i.e., the serpent/Satan), what is more likely in view is the idea of maintaining the garden's beauty and fruitfulness. God created the world needing the human race to interact with it and preserve it. Of course, God could do this activity directly, but He has chosen to use man as His instrument to this end.

There is a wonderful balance in the twin commands to "tend" and "keep" the garden. If the human race rashly tries to draw too much from the creation too quickly or makes transformative changes to the original creation order too abruptly, he may diminish the earth's fruitfulness and abrogate his calling to protect the garden. On the other hand, if Mankind was to act like a museum curator, zealously preserving the creation in its natural, pristine state, he would fail to reap from the earth the resources needed for his continued existence; creation's hidden potentialities would be left buried and unused (Matt. 25:25). Wisdom is required to balance the dual tasks of working and keeping the earth, to avoid the dual pitfalls of overdevelopment and cultural slothfulness.

Man demonstrates that he was created in the image of God through the faithful execution of his culturative calling. The Shorter Catechism elsewhere states that "God executes his decrees in the works of creation and providence," and that "God's works of providence are his . . . preserving and governing all his creatures and all their actions" (Q&A 8, 11). Thus, God's interaction with His creation may be summarized as His acts of "creation," "preserving," and "governing." These three divine activities correspond to those tasks which man performs in his culturative relationship to earth. (The fourth task—filling—is infrastructural; it facilitates the others.) In turn, these foundational, *"earthy"* tasks parallel the threefold calling of mankind to be prophet, priest, and king:

God's Work	Man's Corresponding Cultural Task
creation	tend/work the garden (prophet)
preserving	keeping/guarding (priest)
governing	subduing/dominion (king)

Culture-making is fundamental to man's identity as a creature. This is especially borne out in his profound relationship with the ground/earth, expressed etymologically in the Hebrew names for man (*adam*) and the earth (*adamah*), which have for their root *adom*—"to be red." Note how the interplay (both verbally and relationally) between the ruddy man and the red ground/earth is expressed repeatedly in the opening chapters of Genesis (the repeated use of *abad* ("to work") is also highlighted):

Gen. 2:5: "and there was no man [*adam*] to till [*abad*] the ground [*adamah*]."

Gen. 2:7: "And the LORD God formed the man [*adam*] of the dust of the ground [*adamah*]."

Gen. 2:15: "Then the LORD God took the man [*adam*] and put him in the Garden of Eden to tend [*abad*] and keep it."

Gen. 3:23: "therefore the LORD God sent him out of the Garden of Eden, to till [*abad*] the ground [*adamah*] from which he was taken."

Gen. 4:2: "but Cain was a tiller [*abad*] of the ground [*adamah*]."

Gen. 4:12: (to Cain) "When you till [*abad*] the ground [*adamah*], it shall no longer yield its fruit to you."

Gen. 4:14: "Surely you have driven me out this day from the face of the ground [*adamah*]."

Man was originally taken from the ground, and it seems he was specially created to interact with his namesake through cultivation and culturative acts. Even after the Fall, this vital "working" relationship remains central to what it means to be human. In fact, the sting of God's punishment meted out on Cain is Cain's total estrangement from the ground, leaving him a "groundless" wanderer upon the earth. It may be said, then, that mankind is most at home when he is engaged in cultural activities—when he is free to interact with the earth: guiding and shaping the marvelous raw material from which man himself was taken and shaped.

5.

The scope and richness of God's culturative program for man implies and necessitates the involvement of a community of people with varied functions and abilities. Differentiation and specialization in culturative tasks are inescapable as societies mature and will normally lead to a governing order and a cultural elite.

The nature of man is richly diversified. There is not only a diversity of basic need but there is also a profuse variety of taste and interest, of aptitude and endowment, of desires to be satisfied and of pleasures to be gratified. When we consider the manifold ways in which the earth is fashioned and equipped to meet and gratify the diverse nature and endowments of man, we can catch a glimpse of the vastness and variety of the task involved in subduing the earth, a task directed to the end of developing man's nature, gifts, interests, and powers in engagement with the resources deposited by God in the earth and the sea.

—John Murray, *Principles of Conduct*

The culturative program God assigned to man was comprehensive. Man was to assert his rule lovingly over every living creature as he came to gradually populate the whole surface of the earth. He was also called dually to "work" and "keep" the

Aesthetic Poverty

When we ordinarily speak of poverty and its opposite, wealth, we do so in economic terms. To be rich is to have an accumulation of money and property; to be poor is to have lack of the same. The Bible repeatedly warns that inactivity and laziness will lead to poverty but diligent hard work will lead to material prosperity (Prov. 10:4; 14:23; 19:15, 24:30–34; 28:19; etc.). This is not to say that the diligent will not encounter occasional economic difficulty, or that the lazy will never have riches, although usually for a short time (Prov. 20:21). Material goods flow out of a wise interaction with the earth and its resources, as it is blessed by the Lord (Deut. 8:18). When human beings refuse to or are kept from working the earth, or when God withholds the fruitfulness of the land (Is. 7:23–25; Jer. 12:13), then poverty ensues.

There are other kinds of poverty, as well. America, for all its economic affluence, is in many respects starving when it comes to genuine cultural development, especially in

original paradise, maintaining the earth's rich vitality and fruitfulness while at the same time unlocking the earth's "buried" potential. Man was to use his imagination and skills to transform nature into a glorious garden-city. To the original couple this task must have looked like a thrilling opportunity to be taken on with worshipful joy—along with every other human activity received from the hand of the Maker.

The wide-ranging scope of man's culturative calling reveals another important facet of human life (and, as some theologians have proposed, another aspect of the *imago dei*): the necessity of *community*. This is most obvious in the case of our task to fill the earth—"It is not good that the man should be alone" (Gen. 2:18). Adam, by himself, could not fulfill the command to be fruitful and multiply. He needed a "suitable [i.e., complementary] helper," one who was ideally fitted to assist him in this task. It was clearly evident that the animals, though able to help with some things, were unable to help the man complete his mission comprehensively (Gen. 2:19–20). What was needed was a woman—a fellow "bone of my bones/flesh of my flesh" human being—to enable the man to do his job. On the level of filling the earth, at least, human community was absolutely necessary.

But the need for human community does not end with procreation. Transforming the earth is a complex, multifaceted activity requiring an equally wide-ranging array of skills and talents. Not every culturative activity utilizes the same gifts. The set of skills that makes a gold prospector effective at his job will not necessarily make for a good goldsmith. The talents required of a vinedresser are very different from those of a winetaster. Although it is not entirely clear how the diversity of talents would have been distributed in a world without sin (the Fall came on too quickly for us to know how this would have played out), it is clear that since the Fall, God has chosen to assign to each person differing gifts and talents—both in type and degree—in order to facilitate the sheer breadth of the culturative program.

Immediately after the expulsion from the garden, after the man and the woman had fallen into sin, we see vocational specialization: "Abel was a keeper of the sheep, but Cain was a tiller of the ground" (Gen. 4:2). The text does not reveal why each brother took on the occupation that he did. It could have been that they had innate abilities which suited them to the particular type of job they chose, or it could have been simply preference. (Maybe their father chose for them!) What is clear is that they chose two different occupations which were both related to the themes of "dominion" and "working" developed in Genesis 1 and 2. These differences came into bold relief when the appointed time came for them to bring their offerings to the LORD. Each made his presentation from the fruit of his labors, but one was accepted by God, the other rejected. This made Cain very angry. One possible solution for Cain would have been for him to barter with his brother, trading some of his grain for one of Abel's lambs. Thus, there would have been the beginning not only of the division

the arts. This is not to say that there isn't much to choose from. The book, music, and media superstores have their shelves stuffed with a dizzying array of items to buy with our abundance of disposable income. Some of what's out there possesses genuine depth and quality and is truly worthy to be termed *high* culture. But the rest coalesces into a vast sea of palatable mediocrity—the superabundant effluence of the engines of popular culture. (Folk culture still exists, but it is harder to find and is all too often rapidly assimilated by and packaged into popular culture, making it effectively sterile in the process.) We are very much like the huddled survivors on a lifeboat, dying of thirst in the middle of the vast, useless cultural ocean.

How did we get this way? The answer is a complex one, but it boils down to the radical egalitarianism that is at the core of the American "democratic" ethos, which came into its own in the nineteenth century. Americans have traditionally cast bold aspersion against the cultural elite and, in the process, have cut themselves off from potential sources of intellectually and aesthetically enriching artifacts. This, combined with a "bottom-line" pragmatism, has left us open to the ravages of popular culture, which is driven by marketing and the mass media. One way out of this predicament is to accept the inevitability of an elite class of God-gifted individuals whose job it is to *serve* the rest of society by crafting texts, objects, and structures of real (not pretended) depth and substance. We must also take the time and resources to be educated on the conventions and nuances of high culture and refined artifacts, so that we may reap the full benefits which are there to be enjoyed. This in turn will enable us to appreciate in new ways the riches of folk culture as well.

of labor but of commerce as well. Tragically, history did not turn in that direction and violence ensued. After killing his brother, Cain was permanently alienated from the soil and had no other recourse but to seek relief from his wanderings by building a city (Gen. 4:17). He could not draw life from the earth, but he could gather up the earth's materials and fashion dwellings. Even though Cain was cut off from cultivating the earth, he was not entirely without culturative abilities. He was also able to fulfill his procreative calling. From Cain's line come the sons of Lamech (Gen. 4:19ff), who branched out into a number of (apparently) new culturative ventures: ranching, music, and smithing. Sadly, this strand of culturative development is met with even more sin and violence. And so we come face to face with the simultaneous themes of culturative development and the increase of wickedness (cf. Gen. 11); the latter of which points to the need for redemption.

It is within the very heart of OT redemptive history that we see culturative specialization truly come into its own. During the construction of the tabernacle and the Solomonic temple, God called specific gifted individuals to lead the effort: Bezalel and Aholiab in the case of the tabernacle, and Hiram in the case of the temple. (There were many other individuals who were gifted by God for the task as well, e.g., Ex. 36:1.) Of Bezalel it is said that God "has filled him with the Spirit of God, in wisdom and understanding, in knowledge and manner of all workmanship" (Ex. 35:31; cf. 1 Kgs. 7:14). The variety of occupations used in the building of the tabernacle and temple is astounding: lumbermen, carpenters, spinners, dyers, weavers, embroiderers, seamstresses, foundry workers and metallurgists, goldsmiths, engravers, jewelers, tanners, perfumers, quarry workers, and stone masons. Then there were those who provided direct logistical support: tool makers, keepers of draft animals, seafarers, and laborers. In addition to the craftsmen and laborers, there were those who were involved in the worship activities after the sanctuaries were completed: priests and attendants, musicians, singers, musical instrument makers, and psalmists. The gracious circumstances of OT redemption are a resounding celebration of vocational diversity and human skill. The tabernacle and temple were both emblematic—on a small scale—of the grand diversity which was to mark the global culturative endeavor given to man in the Garden of Eden. And they point forward to the wondrous culturative potentialities which will be released after the consummation, when a glorified, sinless humanity fulfills with perfection the culturative development of the New Earth.

It is important to the development of a culturally mature society that the differences in gifting and skill be clearly recognized, utilized, and celebrated. To fail to accept that God has in fact "built in" these differences within human communities leads either to futility and burnout as one tries to do the whole thing oneself or to the mediocrity which ensues when we fail to acknowledge the superior talents of the few and insist that all should have equal participation in every facet of culture-making. As T. S. Eliot observed in *Notes on the Definition of Culture,* the differences in talent and calling result in a necessary stratification of society:

> Among the more primitive societies, the higher types exhibit more marked differentiations of function amongst their members than the lower types. At a higher stage still, we find that some functions are more honoured than others, and this division promotes the development of *classes,* in which higher honour and privilege are accorded, not merely to the person as functionary but as a member of the class. And the class itself possesses a function, that of maintaining that part of the total culture of the society which pertains to that class. We have to try to keep in mind, that in a healthy society this maintenance of a particular level of culture is

to the benefit, not merely of the class that maintains it, but of the society as a whole. Awareness of this fact will prevent us from supposing that the culture of a "higher" class is something superfluous to society as a whole, or the majority, and from supposing that it is something to be shared equally with all other classes. (p. 107)

When a culture refuses to affirm that God does distribute differing types and degrees of gifts to individuals and fails to allow the gifted to coalesce into an elite group, the inevitable result will be cultural impoverishment. As Eliot elsewhere pointed out in *Notes,* the elite group or class should never ascend the ivory tower and lose touch with rest of society. Snobbery is a sin. The covenant community is to welcome and celebrate individuals from all classes of society (James 2:1–7; Gal. 3:28). The culturative leaders are to be servants of community at large. All biblical leadership—culturative and otherwise—is to be marked by accountability (especially to God, but also to our neighbors) and the willingness to serve the culture as a whole—not just an elite subset of the whole (Mark 10:42–45). On the other hand, the cultural leaders are not to "dumb down" their works for the masses but are to enrich society as a whole by their excellent works. Culturative leaders, when they execute their calling faithfully under God, are also to be accorded honor (cf. 1 Tim. 4:17).

It seems likely, then, that human civil government is not the result of the fall of mankind but would have been necessary even in a world without sin. (Today it has the additional role of restraining sin—Rom. 13:4.) Civil government would have served as an essential infrastructural agency by which the diverse parts of God's comprehensive culturative program could be coordinated and facilitated. Those with superior gifts and abilities to lead and plan would have governed various segments of human society so that the earth-transformative program could be completed in an excellent, God-glorifying manner. Without the effects of sin, those in leadership would never have "lorded it over" (Mark 10:42) those whom they managed, and the governed would have readily deferred to those with superior gifts and talents. Collaboration and cooperation between the different members of the community would still have been the norm; varying levels of decision-making and responsibility would have been meted out according to the level of gifting apportioned by God. Cultural and civil authorities should thus be seen as a blessing to culture-making, even now in a sinful world. Order and organization are necessary for a culture to mature and to reach the glorious potential set before it to develop the earth into a beautiful garden-city.

6.

Culture manifests itself in varying degrees of expressive intensity, formality, and seriousness. "High" culture generally designates those cultural artifacts self-consciously made for lasting use as objects of intellectual and/or aesthetic contemplation, or for religious veneration/service. "Low" culture designates objects made for common purposes, with a special focus on utility.

> *We are far too easily pleased.*
>
> —C.S. Lewis, "The Weight of Glory"

Not only is there a profound diversity of human skills and occupations which are necessary for man to fulfill his calling to transform the earth from splendid garden to glorious city, but there is a correspondingly amazing assortment of products which are the result of culturative activity. This diversity is more than a matter of differing categories of artifacts, types of materials employed, functions met, etc. It also exceeds the variety due to differences of ethnicity, class, or other social categories. The diversity of human culturative products is also a result of the basic approach taken in making artifacts and their position and importance to the community which made them. Mature, healthy societies do not treat all texts, buildings, and man-made objects

The Brussels Sprouts Syndrome

Ask most people in America today, and I suspect that they would tell you that they are *not* fond of brussels sprouts. They may well tolerate or even like other vegetables—peas, carrots, corn, potatoes, and the like—but brussels sprouts are manifestly not favored by the masses. The flavor is simply too intense (and this is putting it kindly). Yet there are many individuals who very much like this small cabbage-like vegetable, do not see the eating of it as some sort of culinary masochism, and wonder what all the fuss is about. Such people speak of brussels sprouts as an "acquired taste," one that takes some prolonged work to learn to enjoy. This kind of sentiment comes off as snobbery to those who have not yet made the effort.

Compare this, for example, to cotton candy. Cotton candy is marvelously entertaining stuff. The puffy, weightless quality of it, the way it seems to melt away to nothing inside your mouth, its sweet, mildly fruity taste—all contribute to

the same. Consider a comparison of an English nursery rhyme with a Japanese *tanka*. While both are short poems, often about common, everyday subjects, no one would argue that "Little Boy Blue," even with its wry sense of humor and moral pith, carries the gravity and subtle beauty of:

> In the lingering wake
> of the breeze that has scattered
>   the cherry tree's bloom,
> petal wavelets go dancing
> across the waterless sky.
>
> —Ki no Tsurayuki

Though these poems come from two very different cultures, it is readily apparent that the former poem is more informal and less pensive than the latter. This does mean that "Little Boy Blue" is an unimportant or bad poem. Just the opposite. It functions exceptionally well to introduce children to the rhythms of the English language and uses humor to bring home an important point about the evil effects of sloth. The *tanka* serves a very different role in the society which birthed it. It is a carefully crafted work of art which celebrates the easily overlooked beauty of nature. Tsurayuki's graceful lines invite the reader to think and rethink the message of its words and, in turn, to look at the commonplace elements of a landscape in an entirely new way.

We can see from these two examples that nursery rhymes and *tanka* occupy different places within the cultures which made them. Nursery rhymes are more utilitarian and straightforward in their function. They are to be enjoyed but are hardly meant to be the objects of serious contemplation. On the other hand, *tanka* are more intellectually and aesthetically sophisticated. Because they are more allusive they require greater effort to understand and enjoy. In short we may say that these two poems differ in their expressive intensity. Cultural artifacts which have greater expressive intensity will generally have a higher degree of formal complexity, aesthetic refinement, intellectual development, emotional passion, and utilitarian elegance. They will also be the product of an exceptionally high degree of craftsmanship. Other objects, while not sacrificing good craftsmanship (which should be the norm for *all* the products of a godly culture), will focus on utility. While building a house, a carpenter does not usually meditate on the aesthetics of his hammer (even though it might have a certain beauty); what he cares about is how efficient it is in striking nails into a block of wood. A healthy society will create artifacts of varying degrees of expressive intensity—from the simplest tool to the most complex work of art, reflecting in part the variety found in nature.

This kind of positional stratification of cultural artifacts is based on expressive intensity and is presupposed in Scripture. Paul, for example, matter-of-factly states, "But in a great house there are not only vessels of gold and silver, but also of wood and clay, some for honor and some for dishonor" (2 Tim. 2:20). Lest anyone think that this is simply a matter of the types of materials used, the apostle states elsewhere, "Does not the potter have power over the clay, from the same lump to make one vessel for honor and another for dishonor?"

its popularity. I suspect that everyone who encounters cotton candy for the first time thoroughly enjoys the experience. But if one were to have a steady diet of cotton candy, would one not quickly grow tired of it—even though it would be generally non-offensive? In this regard, we may say that cotton candy has a *superficial* character; it is definitely delightful at first, but the law of diminishing returns takes effect very quickly. Yet there is nothing wrong with the fact that it is so easily enjoyed, even for a short time, and that it is still fun to eat the rare times that we get to have it. On the other hand, brussels sprouts, even though they are difficult to appreciate the first time they are eaten, are, when one learns to enjoy them, rarely found to be boring even when eaten repeatedly. Their complex, rich character is not easily exhausted.

Culturative artifacts work much the same way as food. Most human works that are part of "high" culture—classical string quartets, for example—are not easily enjoyed at first. One must learn how to perceive them, to know something of the structure of the form, to tune into the subtlety of the work, in order to fully appreciate what is presented. Yet such an effort will be richly rewarded. For each time we encounter such artifacts, we will notice some new aspect of the work which leads to a fresh enjoyment of it. Most artifacts from popular culture do not have this lasting quality. We can all think of a pop song that sounded great the first time we heard it, but after hearing it *ad nauseum* on the radio, we came to hate it after only a short time. Truly great culturative artifacts—like great foods—are both easily accessible and have the depth of character to be encountered time after time and still retain their ability to delight and entertain. Such works are rare but are always prized.

(Rom. 9:21; cf. Is. 44:15–17). Paul utilizes the positional stratification of cultural objects to illustrate theological truths. Hellenistic culture fussed quite a bit over its fine pottery, taking great care to decorate these with finely detailed figural paintings of various subjects. Everyday household vessels were simple earthenware objects accented—if at all—with modest geometric designs.

Human works which are particularly intricate, beautiful, and/or intellectually profound are usually accorded a special kind of honor within the society where they were produced and form the core content of what the community passes on to succeeding generations. In many cases these expressively rich works are tied to the religious life of the community and are objects which might even contribute to the community's sense of identity. Such objects, when taken together as a class of artifacts, are often referred to as "high" culture: "high" because they have traditionally been associated with the more affluent, better-educated classes of society (although there have been exceptions to this rule—Renaissance Florence to name one) and because they tend to investigate and give expression to the core truths and values of a community's worldview (i.e., deal with the "big" questions of life). In developing expressively rich artifacts, man also has the opportunity to self-consciously respond to the awesome magnificence of the Creator and His creation. Human beings were made to dwell upon those things which are true, noble, just, pure, lovely, virtuous, and excellent (Phil. 4:8) and to incorporate these praiseworthy elements into their culturative works. This may result in something as subtle as the shine of reflected light in the leather of a child's shoe or the overpowering rhythms and spaces of a soaring cathedral. Even so, we would be mistaken to assume that "high" culture is intrinsically better or more necessary to a community's cultural fabric, as we shall see shortly (indeed, one of the tragedies of contemporary Western culture is the bankrupt nature of much that passes for high culture).

In addition to "high" culture, we may speak of two categories of "low" culture or the assortment of common, everyday artifacts used by the whole community. Such objects, texts, and structures are often beautiful in their own right and may express important ideas, but their overall focus is on utility. "Folk" culture refers to the artifacts created by a certain group or "folk" sharing common ethnic and religious ties. Because such works only have to "function" for the group, the objects of "folk" culture often have an expressive integrity and clarity which other types of cultural objects do not possess. Folk culture is the most basic, traditional, and ubiquitous form of cultural expression. "Popular" culture, by contrast, is a modern phenomenon which attempts to be the cultural expression of many (if not all) "folks" within a pluralistic society. The products created by popular culture, in their attempt to appeal to a wide range of communities, form a culture of the "lowest common denominator" and hence have a shallow, ephemeral character compared to the integrity of folk culture, which only has to be true for the group. A comparison of the three modes of culture can be summarized as follows (Compare this list to that of Ken Myers in *All God's Children and Blue Suede Shoes*, p. 120; my analysis of folk, pop, and high culture owes much to Myer's deft observations.):

Folk Culture	*Popular Culture*	*High Culture*
home cooking	McDonald's	gourmet cuisine
square dancing	disco	ballet
Negro spiritual	Beatles	symphony
fairy tale	mystery novel	*War & Peace*
bib overalls	Dockers™	tuxedo

It should be noted that many cultural works transcend the boundaries outlined above. Mark Twain's *Huckleberry Finn* and *Tom*

Sawyer can safely be said to reside in the realm of high culture; nevertheless, they have always had a wide appeal. And many would say that the Beatles at times transcended the boundaries of popular and high culture. One of the problems with popular culture is its tendency to appropriate motifs from folk and high culture for its own mass-market purposes, often rendering the original artifact or idea expressively impotent in the process.

All highly developed cultures have artifacts which fall into the various cultural strata described here. (Healthier cultures avoid the deadening effects of popular culture.) Mature cultures—those which have adopted a high degree of complexity, both vocationally and in terms of the types of objects, texts, and structures they have developed—will have the requisite skills and tools required to undertake the transformative process in all its comprehensive glory. Man—the divine image-bearer—was called to imitate the gloriously diverse splendor of God's creation with cultural works of his own, which in manifold ways celebrate, reflect, and glorify our Father's majestic Name (Ps. 8:9).

PART TWO:

CULTURE AND REDEMPTION

Mankind's mission to transform the earth through culture-making was radically altered—but not abandoned—by the entrance of sin into the world. The Fall made the human race rebel against God's righteous commands, including the command to rule and work the creation. Nevertheless, fallen mankind was still capable of some culturative good. Man was now the object of God's holy wrath. A perfect sacrifice was needed so that mankind could be reconciled to the Father. This salvation was secured through the incarnate Son of God—Jesus Christ. Man could now be restored to a state of holiness so that he could return to his calling to rule, fill, work, and keep the creation. The future hope of God's people is eternal life on the glorious, restored New Earth, where culture will flourish without the detrimental effects of sin, and the best and most noble of human cultural artifacts will furnish the holy Jerusalem.

7.

Redemptive history is God's unfolding purpose for man to make a covenanted people for Himself from the fallen, sinful human race. The ultimate purpose of redemptive history is restoring mankind to holiness of body and soul *in order* that God's original culturative program may be fulfilled with joyful obedience.

> *To affirm and bask in the goodness of the world, to praise God for the wonders of creation, to practice responsible stewardship of this small planet, and to honor its Maker by using its resources wisely for the welfare of the race and the enriching of human life are all integral aspects of the work that Christians are called to do. Any idea that consistent Christianity must undermine or diminish concern for the tasks of civilization should be dismissed once and for all.*
>
> —J. I. Packer and Thomas Howard,
> *Christianity: The True Humanism*

In the beginning, all that God created on the earth was *good* (Gen. 1:31). This included the capstone of His creation, man (Gen. 1:26ff). Everything from the hand of the Maker—all the animals, all the plant life, all the natural processes acting on inanimate matter, and all the thoughts, decisions, and actions of man-

David and Solomon: Two Kingly Types

Even though their two personalities and reigns were remarkably different, King David and his royal son Solomon were both striking types of Christ, prefiguring different aspects of Jesus' messianic ministry. The reign of David was a picture of the king-as-warrior, picturing the Messiah's role as a conqueror of His enemies and a vindicator of His people (Ps. 72; 110:1). In David we see the principle of *the antithesis:* good struggling against and finally triumphing over evil. This is a key component of redemptive history.

Solomon was the opposite of his father. His name said it all: he was a man of peace (*shalom*-on). The contrast of father and son is revealed in David's words of 1 Chronicles 22:7–10:

> It was in my mind to build a house to the name of the LORD, but the word of the LORD came to me, saying, "You have shed much blood and made great wars; you shall not build a house for My name.... Behold a son shall be born to you, who shall be a man of

kind—functioned just as it was meant to function: in total harmony and *shalom,* without evil inclination, entirely directed toward and focused on glorifying God (Ps. 19). Man the image-bearer, being a creature endowed with the capacity to *self-consciously* do his works to the glory of God, fulfilled his calling to fill, rule, work, and keep the creation flawlessly, without the slightest hint of hesitation, complaint, or self-aggrandizement. He thoroughly *enjoyed* serving his Creator. This is the way it was in the beginning. But the creation did not stay that way for long.

Sin changed everything. One could say that, strictly speaking, sin entered the world in the form of a cunning serpent. He set about his subversive task immediately, confronting the woman with the prospect that God is a liar (Gen. 3:1–4). If the man and woman had fulfilled their calling to guard ("keep") the creation properly (Gen. 2:15), they would have recognized the perverse intent of the intruder and crushed his head right then and there. But they did not. First the woman and then the man doubted the word of the LORD, ate the prohibited fruit of the tree of the knowledge of good and evil and, just as God proclaimed, brought death to themselves and to all their posterity. The open fellowship and *shalom* which the first couple had with their Creator and with each other was broken. This is symbolized by the fig-leaf coverings they made for themselves (before this, they were "naked ... and were not ashamed"—Gen. 2:25) and their vain attempt to hide from God (Gen. 3:7–8).

Yet even in midst of this tragedy of tragedies, there was still hope. The effects of sin could be reversed, but only at a great price. The man and the woman did not die physically the moment the fruit touched their lips. The sovereign Creator revealed that He is a longsuffering God, willing to endure for a while the sin of His creatures because He has a greater purpose in mind for the human race. This purpose is hinted at in Genesis 3:15: "And I will put enmity between you [the serpent] and the woman, and between your seed and her seed; He shall bruise your head and you shall bruise His heel." From the seed of the woman a *New* Adam would emerge (Rom. 5:12ff), who through His own suffering would crush the head of the serpent and at the same time serve as a bloody sacrifice for the redemption of a restored humanity. We see the necessity for sacrifice first foretold by the animal skin garments which the LORD provided as a covering for the man and the woman (Gen. 3:21). Sacrifice continues to be the prescribed means for securing fellowship with God in the rest of the OT; it is practiced both by the ancient fathers (Gen. 4:4; 8:20; 13:18; 26:25; 33:20) and the Aaronic priesthood (Lev., *passim*). All of this points to Jesus Christ.

Why did God the Father send his incarnate Son to the cross to die? The apostle John plainly tells us the answer: "In this the love of God was manifested toward us, that God sent His only begotten Son into the world, that we might live through Him. In this is love, not that we loved God, but that He loved us and sent His Son to be a propitiation for our sins" (1 Jn. 4:9–10). As a *propitiation* for our sins, Christ satis-

rest. . . . His name shall be Solomon, for I will give peace and quietness to Israel in his days. He shall build a house for My name."

After David had routed his enemies within the borders of Israel, he was able to rest from his labors and turn the kingdom over to his son (1 Kgs. 5:3–4). Thus Solomon's reign prefigures the eternal reign of Christ over the New Heavens and the New Earth (Rev. 22) after the defeat of God's enemies. The ensuing peace was a time of great culturative activity for the Jewish people. Indeed, Solomon was the paradigmatic culturative man. Besides heading up the building of the temple, Solomon used his God-given wisdom for a vast array of culturative pursuits (2 Chr. 8:1–9:28; Eccl. 2:4–8; not to mention his brilliant literary works).

In the kingdoms of David and Solomon we see an important principle which governs the relationship between redemptive and culturative history. Redemptive history—marked by either the conversion or the destruction of God's enemies, and eradication of evil and sin—paves the way for culturative progress to be carried out by God's people. Thus we read in Isaiah 2:4 that "they shall beat their swords into plowshares, /And their spears into pruning hooks." The weapons of war (antithesis) shall be transformed into tools for farming (the paradigm for culture-making), which hearkens us back to Adam's original vocation to rule and work the earth, in the opening chapters of Genesis.

fied the righteous requirements of God's justice upon the sins of men and women (Rom. 3:25f) by being a perfect, spotless Lamb led to the slaughter. Since Jesus was God, He was able to quench the entirety of the Father's infinite wrath and still be victorious, rising from the dead as a bold demonstration of God's saving power. On the basis of Christ's death, the Father willed that many would believe, and thereby have "the right to become children of God" (John 1:12–13).

For what purpose did God make us to be His redeemed children? What are we to do with our newfound status before our loving adoptive Father? Many would say that Christ died so that the elect may have the opportunity to fellowship with God. Others would propose that His sacrifice was to give us new hearts that would willingly desire to worship God and to lead a holy life. Some would answer that we were redeemed in order that we might go out and preach the gospel, converting others and discipling them. While all of these describe what truly happens to the children of God, they do not adequately focus on the *end* of salvation. We must ask the crucial question: What is it that we are saved *unto*?

The answer to this question is wonderfully summarized in the first two chapters of Ephesians. First, Paul tells us that we were redeemed in order that we might receive an *inheritance:* "In Him we have obtained an inheritance, being predestined according to Him who works all things according to the counsel of His will" (1:11; cf. 1:14; 1:18; 3:6; Acts 20:32; Col. 3:24). Why do we have this inheritance coming to us? Because our Father has "predestined us to the adoption as sons by Jesus Christ to Himself" (1:5). Because of our adopted status before God in Christ, we have the legal right to our inheritance.

This leaves us with the all-important question: What is the inheritance? The apostle hints at this in Ephesians 6:2–3: "'Honor your father and mother,' which is the first commandment with a promise: 'that it may be well with you and you may live long on the *earth*.'" Here we see a remarkable shift in focus from God's original wording of the fifth commandment found in Exodus and Deuteronomy. The original promise was that obedient covenant children were to live long upon "the land which the LORD your God is giving you" (Ex. 20:12; Deut. 5:16). The Israelites were to receive the inheritance promised to their father Abraham (Gen. 13:4–5). Paul now informs us that *all* true believers—Jew and non-Jew—are sons of Abraham (Gal. 3:7ff; Rom. 4:11–12) and "heirs according to the promise" (Gal. 3:25; cf. Rom. 8:17). The promised inheritance which is ours because of our adoption as sons, which originally was confined to the region west of the Jordan River and the Dead Sea, is now revealed in Ephesians 6:3 to be the whole earth! "Blessed are the meek, for they shall inherit *the earth*" (Matt. 5:5; cf. Ps. 37:11). The writer of Hebrews tells us that Abraham was looking forward to "the city which has foundations, whose builder and maker is God" (11:10) and that the OT saints set their hope on arriving at "a heavenly country," that God has "prepared a city for them" (11:16; cf. 12:22, 13:14). What seems to be in view here is the New Earth and the New Jerusalem of Revelation 21 and 22. All true believers will "live long" (indeed forever!) on *the earth* (i.e., the New Earth), which we will receive from our Father as our long-promised inheritance.

In addition to our inheritance, Paul tells us the other end for which we were redeemed: "For we are his workmanship, created in Christ Jesus *for good works,* which God prepared beforehand that we should walk in them" (Eph. 2:10). While we are not able to merit salvation through good works, our works are nevertheless an indispensable part of the life of all true believers, as the NT makes abundantly clear:

All scripture is given by inspiration of God, and is profitable for doctrine, for reproof, for correction, for instruction in righteousness, that the man of God may be equipped for *every good work*. (2 Tim. 3:16–17)

For this reason we also . . . do not stop praying for you, and to ask that you may be filled with the knowledge of His will in all wisdom and spiritual understanding, that you may walk worthy of the Lord, fully pleasing Him, being fruitful in *every good work*. (Col. 1:9–10)

Now may the God of peace, who brought up our Lord Jesus from the dead, that great Shepherd of the sheep, through the blood of the everlasting covenant, make you complete in *every good work* to do His will, working in you what is pleasing in His sight. (Heb. 13:20–21)

Therefore, my beloved brethren, be steadfast, immovable, always abounding in *the work* of the Lord, knowing that your labor is not in vain. (1 Cor. 15:58)

Let your light shine before men, that they may see your *good works* and glorify your Father in heaven. (Matt. 5:16)

Most Christians, when they read these and similar passages, think that "good works" refer to specific acts of kindness or service, perhaps rendered to those who are spiritually or economically needy. While this sense of "works" is partly in view, it must be argued that a broader idea of work is intended. The Greek word rendered "work" (and sometimes as "deed") in these passages of the NT is *ergon* (from which we get the term ergonomics). This is the same word used in the Septuagint to translate the Hebrew *abad* in chapters 2–4 of Genesis (see previous discussion). Adam, before the Fall, was called to *work* the garden in all joy, glorifying the LORD. After the Fall, work continued, but in weakness and frustration, often decidedly against the will of the Creator (e.g., Gen. 11). Indeed, much of the work of sinful man is done in vain (Eccl. 1). But in the case of those whom God restores to a new life of faith, their works—culturative as well as restorative and evangelistic—are certainly not done in vain (Ps. 127:1), but it is Yahweh, our covenanting Father, who will "establish the work of our hands" (Ps. 90:17; cf. Hebrews 13:20–21 quoted above). This is the context of the so-called "Great Commission" of Matthew 28:18–20. The Church is to go out into the whole world to make disciples who will obey *all* of God's commands (v. 19). Thus God seeks to create a community of redeemed men and women who are to be equipped for *every* good work. *We are redeemed so that we may work!* The human race is brought back to a state of righteousness so that we might return to our Edenic calling to develop ("work") *the earth* into a glorious garden-city and finally take possession of our long-awaited inheritance.

Returning to Genesis 3, we learn that sin did not only estrange man from God and from his fellow man but also brought estrangement from the earth. In fact, Paul tells us that the creation violently groans under the curse of God because of man's transgression (Rom. 8:19ff). Now, drawing out the hidden potentialities residing in the earth will no longer be easy. Men will have to strive with "thorns and thistles" and gain the fruit of the earth only "by the sweat of your brow" (Gen. 3:18–19). Likewise, verse 16 informs us that the task of filling the earth will now be accompanied by increased pain in childbirth. Yet even in this there is hope: the call to fill, rule, work, and keep the earth is not rescinded. Children are born (Gen. 4:1). Man is still able to make the earth bring forth its fruit, however grudgingly (Gen. 4:3). But just as God's covenant people have been freed from their slavery to sin so that they can fulfill their culturative tasks to God's glory and will one day themselves be glorified (Rom. 8:18), so the earth too will find release from its bondage at the very same time that the glory of the saints is fully revealed! (Rom. 8:21). The works we are able to perform now by the empowerment of the Holy Spirit (Rom. 8:11ff) are the firstfruits of the works we will do in our future life after we have been fully sanctified and glorified (Rom. 8:23). We therefore have a great hope that we will be able now and in the future to fulfill the commandment that was set before us in the Garden of Eden to transform the earth.

8.

Since culturative history was inaugurated by God before the fall of Adam, it is to be seen as a basic, integral, and (potentially) holy calling of mankind. Fallen man continues to participate in God's culturative program by means of God's common grace. Believers are further empowered by the Holy Spirit to perform their cultural calling self-... y of God.

... in the total development toward ...nd power over nature gradually ...uardianship of 'common grace.' ...s work, that unfolds here. It was ...' humanity with all these powers. ...he seed which lay hidden in that ...ne up and blossomed. Thanks to ...ed, burgeoned, shot up high and ...ower, to reward not man but the ...finished world will glorify God ...reme Craftsman. What paradise ...n bud will appear in full bloom.

—Abraham Kuyper, *Common Grace*

The human race was called to fill, rule, work, and keep the earth *before* the Fall—before sin and evil had ever entered the hearts, thoughts, and actions of men and women. Man's culturative activities must therefore be seen as a normative, good, and holy calling received from a loving and holy God. Marriage, work, the development of the earth's resources, and a careful stewardship of nature must all be seen as intrinsic to who we are. It is clear from the rest of Scripture that our culturative calling was never rescinded after the Fall (e.g., Gen. 4; 9:1–2). The entrance of sin into the world has, however, drastically complicated the historical picture, bringing an additional, ethical dimension into view. Now, in addition to the *culturative* strand of history, we have *redemptive* history as well. The relationship between culturative and redemptive history is schematically pictured in figure 2 (compare this to figure 1 on page 32).

Figure 2: The dual dimensions of human history after the Fall.

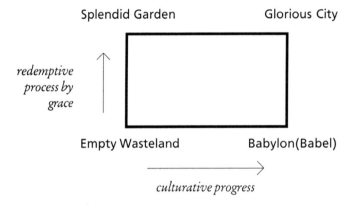

Before the Fall, human history simply involved the gradual culturative transformation of the earth over time from a beautiful garden to a glorious city. After the Fall, sin introduced a new set of variables to the historic panorama. Now, the pristine, splendid garden could be ruined on account of man's sinful choices and actions. What was once fruitful and beautiful could be turned into a barren, empty wasteland (Jer. 4:23–29; Rev. 11:18). Yet fallen man, even left to his sinful, perverse devices, is still able to effect culturative changes to the earth, albeit in a warped manner, with rebellious motives (Gen. 4). The Fall has radically affected all aspects of our person—body and soul, intellect, emotions, and will (Rom. 1:18ff; 3:10ff; Eph. 4:17–19)—yet in God's providence, sin is restrained and fallen man is able to do outward acts of kindness, goodness, and beauty, including positive culturative acts. We may even assert that the culturative products of non-Christian civilizations are sometimes of great value (Matt. 4:8). The Westminster Confession summarizes the Bible's teaching this way:

> Works done by unregenerate men, although . . . they may be things which God commands and of good use both to themselves and others; yet, because they do not proceed from a heart purified by faith; . . . nor to a right end, the glory of God; they are therefore sinful and cannot please God. . . . And yet their neglect of them is more sinful, and displeasing unto God. (chap. 16.7)

John Murray wryly remarks on the closing words of this section, "The ploughing of the wicked is sin [Prov. 22:4, AV], but it is more sinful for the wicked not to plough."

After the Fall, the *imago dei* in mankind was not obliterated, but it was greatly distorted. Man continues in the culturative tasks originally assigned to him by God before the Fall, but now they are performed out of unholy motives and at their core are sinful acts, even though superficially they may be of some benefit. Marriages still produce offspring, but the children are now corrupted by sin and are agents of evil (Ps. 51:5; 58:3; Deut. 28:18). Godly rule over the animals often devolves into cruel exploitation. The balance between working and keeping the earth is lost, resulting in overdevelopment and destruction of the earth's fruitfulness. Apart from God's redemptive intervention, it is a very bleak picture indeed; nevertheless, some culturative progress is possible.

The repeatedly used biblical type for the civilization of the ungodly is Babylon (Is. 13–14; Rev. 18), which had its initial origins in the city of Babel (Gen. 10:10; 11:1–9). *Babel* (*confusion* in Hebrew) is the result of man's conspiratorial efforts against God (cf. Ps. 2), creating a counterfeit culture which has many of the external trappings of a godly human civilization but is at its core self-consciously directed against the culturative commandments of the LORD (Gen. 11:4). Redemption is often pictured as the liberation from Babylon (confusion) to Jerusalem (Yahweh's peace), as in Psalm 126 (cf. Gen. 11:31). Jerusalem is simultaneously a paradigm for the whole Promised Land as well as a type of the New Jerusalem which is to come. Redemption is not pictured as a return to the pristine garden but as a move from one city polluted by sin and idols to another, radically different city characterized by holiness and the presence of God. The redeemed are not called to abandon culture per se but to flee from godless culture so that we may make, participate in, and embrace a *Christian* culture.

At various times in the history of God's people, a proper vision of the relationship between redemptive and culturative history has been lost. During the Medieval era, monasticism was held as the highest ideal. While the legendary industriousness of the monks was a principal force behind the culturative development of Europe, the practice of celibacy was a de facto denial of the normative goodness of marriage and the culturative commandment to fill the earth. Formal worship and prayer were seen to have paramount importance; all else was seen as a diversion from this "highest" of godly callings. The Reformation brought a strong biblical correction to the Medieval understanding of culturative things. Marriage and work in *all* its variety, having been instituted by the Creator before the Fall, were holy callings fit for any child of God to undertake. Moreover, any lawful vocation was seen as a worshipful activity that brings glory to the Father (1 Cor. 10:31). The sacred/secular distinction which was so important to the Medieval conception of society was abolished in the reformational worldview. Luther proclaimed with characteristic boldness, "It looks like a small thing when a maid cooks and cleans and does other housework. But because God's command is there, even such a small work must be praised as a service of God far surpassing the holiness and asceticism of all monks and nuns[!]"

Contemporary western evangelicalism and its more conservative sister movement, fundamentalism, also have a truncated view of the relationship between culturative and redemptive history. In this case, evangelism takes the central position. But (as was discussed previously) what is evangelism for? What are men and women redeemed *unto?* The biblical answer to this question is obscured by the teachings of dispensational premillenialism (the dominant eschatological position of American evangelicals), which specifically assigns man's culturative calling not to the Church but to the Jewish nation. Lewis Sperry Chafer—one of dispensationalism's chief proponents—explained it this way:

> The dispensationalist believes that throughout the ages God is pursuing two distinct purposes: one related to the earth with earthly people and earthly [i.e., culturative] objectives involved, which is Judaism; while the other is related to heaven with heavenly people and heavenly objectives involved, which is Christianity.

O. Palmer Robertson, in responding to the dualism of the dispensational system, sets forth the totality of the scriptural vision for human beings when he states,

> The whole of the Christian faith cries out against such a distinction. Man cannot be partitioned in such a manner because he was not created in such a dualistic fashion. Man was created as a physical/spiritual complex. The only meaningful redemption man can experience is in terms of the renewal of his total being in the context of his total environment.

Christ's incarnation is a bold affirmation of the goodness of physical creation. Jesus assumed human flesh so that he might redeem us, body *and* soul (1 Cor. 15). The holistic character of Christ's ministry of reconciliation should color our understanding of the relationship between culturative and redemptive history. Human beings are graciously restored to a state of holiness of body and spirit so that man's original culturative calling may be fulfilled in true, joyful obedience (Rom. 8:4).

We should therefore expect Christians as a whole to excel in their culturative efforts when compared to those left in their sin. The regeneration of the believer's heart (John 3) introduces a new principle of obedience to the Christian life (Rom. 6). The child of God is no longer bound to chafe at his Father's commands (culturative and otherwise) but now is able to delight in God's law (Rom. 7:22; Ps. 1:2; 119:16, 35). The Christian is further impelled to obedience by the indwelling of the Holy Spirit, who empowers him to walk in God's commandments (Rom. 8), thereby demonstrating his newfound love for his Creator (John 14:15, 21). Fulfilling our calling to fill, rule, work, and keep God's creation is now the Christian's chief joy. Why is it, then, that the Church does not seem to excel more in our culturative efforts? Part of the answer lies in the problem of remaining sin. In this life, before our eventual glorification (Rom. 8:16, 30), when all of the vestiges of sin shall be removed (1 Cor 15:42ff), we must strive by the power of the Holy Spirit to avoid sin and to live a holy life. Failure to mortify the deeds and desires of our sinful nature will result in every kind of ineffectiveness—culturative included. We often fare no better than non-Christians in our culturative pursuits because we really don't live our lives all that differently than they do.

The other reason why on an individual-by-individual basis Christians do not out-perform non-Christians in the culturative arena is because Christians are often not born with exceptional culturative gifts. While the miracle of regeneration allows us to stop sinning and lead a holy life, it is not usually accompanied by new talents. For example, a tone-deaf person who becomes a Christian will still sing out of tune. What regeneration *does* bring to a believer is a newfound motivation to fulfill the talent potential God has already vested in him (Col. 4:23; cf. Eccl. 9:10). Clearly, then, if every Christian across the whole earth was more consistent in pursuing holiness and was working with all his might at the culturative tasks he is well suited for, the result would be vibrant culture made to and for God's glory. May God bring about such a reformation in the hearts of men and women that we might see such a godly culture flourish in our lifetime!

9.

God allows human beings outside His covenant community to prosper in their culturative activities for the ultimate benefit and profit of the Church, His bride. Christians may appropriate some non-Christian objects, forms, and texts for their own culturative ends, but they must do so taking extreme care, ever sensitive to the norms and standards provided in Scripture.

> *Now these are, so to speak, their gold and silver, which they did not create themselves but dug out of the mines of God's providence which are everywhere scattered abroad, and are perversely and unlawfully prostituting to the worship of devils. These therefore the Christian, when he separates himself in spirit from the miserable fellowship of these men ought to take away from them and to devote to their proper use in preaching the gospel. Their garments, also—that is human institutions such as are adopted to that intercourse with men which is indispensable in this life—we must take and turn to a Christian use.*

—Augustine of Hippo, *On Christian Doctrine*

Culturative history continues to unfold after the fall of mankind. Human civilizations have irreversibly altered and added to the original "natural" landscape, sometimes for the better, often for the worse. Yet as pervasive as sin is in the hearts of individuals and in societies at large, man is still able to perform some real good as he undertakes the transformation of the original garden into a garden-city. We would expect communities of redeemed men and women—those who have been healed and restored from the effects of sin—to be able to create striking buildings, beautiful art works, insightful scientific discoveries, etc. And history has shown this to often be true. What is perplexing is the success that non-Christians often have in their culturative efforts—even those cultures which appear never to have been influenced by Judeo-Christian ideas and beliefs. An excellent case in point is ancient Chinese civilization. The Chinese excelled in nearly every area of culturative development: poetry, textiles, papermaking, bronzework, architecture, large-scale agriculture, etc. Two of their achievements are particularly impressive in terms of their grand scale: the Great Wall, stretching almost 3,000 miles, and the expansive Tomb of the First Emperor, containing over 7,000 realistic life-size terra-cotta figurines. Both were completed before 200 B.C. Nevertheless, there is no evidence that ancient China ever had contact with the OT Scriptures or Hebrew ideas.

The question arises: why does God allow non-Christian societies to prosper in their culturative activities? A biblical answer to this question is this: God, in His providence, has repeatedly bestowed a superabundance of culturative gifts to non-Christians, then restrained their evil desires and actions, so that they may make beneficial structures, artifacts, and texts. This gifting does not mean that people outside the covenant are saved. The Bible is clear that non-Christians are without hope in the world (Eph. 2:12) and are the objects of God's wrath (Rom. 9:22) unless they repent and believe on the finished work of Jesus Christ. These cultural gifts (*charisma*) are said to be the result of common grace (grace=*charis*), because they are bestowed by God on Christian and non-Christian alike.

God allows the beneficial cultural works of non-Christians to come into existence so that they may be given over to God's people for *their* use and enjoyment. This reflects a broad scriptural principle. Proverbs 13:22 teaches, "The wealth of the sinner is stored up for the righteous." Ecclesiastes 2:26 states this even more plainly:

> God gives wisdom and knowledge and joy to a man who is good in His sight; but to the sinner He gives the work of gathering and collecting, that he may give to him who is good before God.

God allows those outside His covenant to flourish in their culturative activities so that their ideas, insights, and products may be used by God's people (cf. Prov. 28:8, Job 27:16–17). This is nothing more than the truth that "all things work together for good to those who love God" (Rom. 8:28) playing itself out in culturative history.

This biblical principle was fulfilled many times in OT history. For example, when the Israelites left Egypt, God moved the Egyptians to turn over their goods to the chosen people just before their exodus:

> [35]Now the children of Israel had done according to the word of Moses, and they asked from the Egyptians articles of silver, articles of gold and clothing. [36]And the LORD had given the people favor in the sight of the Egyptians, so that they granted them what they requested. Thus they plundered the Egyptians. (Ex. 12:35–36; also Ex. 3:21–22; 11:1–3)

Undoubtedly, this was the very same gold and silver that was used to make the fittings and vessels used in the tabernacle (Ex. 36ff), which (as discussed previously) was a microcosm of the global garden-city which mankind is in the process of building on the earth. The plundering of the Egyptians had clear culturative (and redemptive) consequences. We see this principle also worked out in the settling of the Promised Land:

> [10]So it shall be, when the LORD brings you into the land of which He swore to your fathers, to Abraham, Isaac and Jacob, to give you large and beautiful cities, which you did not build, [11]houses full of good things, which you did not fill, hewn-out wells which you did not dig, vineyards and olive trees which you did not plant— when you have eaten and are full—[12]then beware, lest you forget the LORD, who brought you out of the land of Egypt, from the house of bondage. (Deut. 6:10–12; cf. Josh. 24:13)

God had used the Canaanites—the epitome of a perverted, pagan society—to begin to develop the culturative potential of the Promised Land. God graciously allowed the Israelites to enjoy the fruits of their enemy's labors!

This same principle is in operation for the Church today. God has placed us in the midst of a civilization of unparalleled culturative development. We now have the knowledge, tools, and raw materials at our disposal to enhance the earth's fruitfulness in ways which could never have been achieved before. The Church must seize the opportunity that the contemporary circumstances present to us and boldly set out to transform the earth, continuing where righteous Adam, before his fall into sin, left off. That the West presently enjoys the degree of culturative success it now has is due to the biblical principles once celebrated by earlier generations and embedded in our cultural fabric. These vestiges of a formerly Christian civilization are now fading away, leaving the preponderance of technology, literature, the arts, etc., to be produced by non-Christian culture-makers, who, as they become more self-conscious and consistent with their anti-Christian stance, will express their unbelief in their artifacts with increasing boldness. Within such a context, "plundering" the plethora of works we find all around us is tricky business. With extreme care, though, believers may appropriate many of these artifacts and use them for godly ends. Let us examine briefly how this might be done.

Our contemporary situation is extremely similar to that which faced the NT Church. How was the NT Church to react to the ungodly Hellenistic culture which challenged it from all sides? The foundational, guiding principle for navigating danger-ridden cultural waters is that the Church is to be "in the world, but not of the world." This principle was most clearly articulated in Christ's "High Priestly" prayer (John 17:9–11,13–19), but it is found throughout the NT (e.g., Rom. 12:2; James 4:4; 1 Jn. 2:15–17). What does this key phrase—especially the two prepositions *in* and *of*—mean? Clearly to be "*in* the world " is to be physically located on the earth in the midst of non-Christians, a place where sin still abounds. Thus Paul says that the only way the Corinthian Christians could completely avoid interaction with non-Christians would be "to go out of the world" (1 Cor. 5:10).

God, in His perfect wisdom, has chosen to leave us here on the earth, for a time. And, as the surrounding culture becomes more hostile, we even begin to feel like we are aliens (1 Pet. 1:1). We are also warned not to be *of* the world." It is clear that "the world" in the second phrase cannot have the same meaning as in the first. If this were the case, being "not of the world" would mean not having interaction with everyday physical, created things, as some ascetic-minded Christians have proposed. This false idea runs counter to other NT passages (Luke 7:34; 1 Tim. 4:4–5) and to the unavoidably *physical* nature of our basic culturative calling. To be "not of the world" is better interpreted as not coming under the influence of the "world system" that is the sum total of actions and beliefs dominated by sin and outside of the redeeming sway of Christ. It is not the creation per se that we are to avoid but *the sin* which presently inhabits God's creation. The challenge for the Christian is how to utilize the cultural goods made by non-Christians without being brought under their influence.

We should first point out that Christian artisans are free to use any basic raw materials (bricks, lumber, paint, sheetmetal, etc.), even those manufactured outside the covenant community. This is the upshot of Paul's teaching on eating food offered to idols (1 Cor. 8:4ff; 10:25ff; cf. Rom. 14): even if food (a basic commodity) is prepared under demonic circumstances (a pagan temple), the believer who has a free conscience has license to partake. We also see this principle in the building of the temple: non-Jews were involved in the preparation of lumber and stone for the holy dwelling (2 Chr. 2:8–10, 18), which were then finished and installed by Israelite craftsmen.

Finished cultural works are more problematic. How are Christians to approach the art works, literature, scientific theories, mathematical proofs, etc. of non-Christians? Are we free to use any style, motif, form, methodology, etc. that we find in our contemporary (or historical) surroundings? It must be recognized that all human works express to some degree the beliefs (worldview) and values of the people who made them (i.e., "culture is religion externalized"). With the objects of "low" culture (e.g., tools, everyday clothing, technological devices), this expressive dimension is relatively restrained, being overridden by utilitarian concerns. Most of these works (but not all!) may be appropriated by the covenant community without compromising one's faith. On the other hand, "high" culture has a more pronounced expressive aspect. Marshall McLuhan's aphorism "the medium is the message" gets to the heart of the matter: the medium (the *means* of expression) and message (*what* is expressed) are *both* inescapably expressive and non-neutral. Christians must be on their guard to evaluate—according to scriptural standards (1 Cor. 2:15; 1 Thess. 5:21f; Phil. 4:8)—the ideological bias of the medium and ideological content of the message of non-Christian (and Christian) artifacts. (We are not free to assume that works made by Christians are *Christian!*) The objects, texts, and structures of the "world" can be a snare to us, just as they were for the Jews as they came into the Promised Land (Deut. 7:16; 12:30). In effect, we must "test the spirit" (cf. 1 Jn. 4:1) of these works to see what, if anything, can be retained and used for godly culture-building. The suggestions Al Wolters provides in his book *Creation Regained* for the analysis of human works by the categories of "structure" and "direction" are especially helpful. A brief article which explains these evaluative tools and provides an example of their use appears as an appendix at the end of this book.

The principle of non-Christian cultural progress being directed by God for the ultimate benefit of His people will have its final fulfillment in the New Jerusalem, when "the glory and honor" of the nations will be ushered into the heavenly garden-city at the end of history (Rev. 21:24, 26). This future event was prefigured by the Magi who brought their token gifts to the infant King of kings (Matt. 2:11; cf. Ps. 72:10). We examine this idea in considerable detail in the next section.

10.

The most noble and excellent of all culturative products will have a place in the New Jerusalem. A joyful affirmation of the future potential of man-made artifacts will lead the redeemed community of God to have a positive outlook on the physical creation and its development by human beings.

If I knew the world was going to end tomorrow, I would plant a tree today.

—Martin Luther

The early chapters of Genesis make it clear that mankind was to fill and rule the whole earth and to utilize his gifts to develop and embellish the original creation. Subsequent revelations from God have provided us with glimpses into what the end results of the culturative process should be like. The ultimate goal and prescriptive pattern toward which our culturative efforts are to be directed is the New Jerusalem—the *perfect* garden-city—which was hinted at, at earlier times in history (Abraham and other OT saints looked forward to it—Heb. 11:10, 16). This future city was prefigured both by the tabernacle and temple (both culturative projects directed toward redemptive ends) as well as the original Jerusalem, which served as the paradigm for all God-governed culturative communities.

Are Christians Still Pilgrims?

The Greek word *parepidemos* is used to describe God's saints in 1 Peter 1:1 and 2:11. This term (appearing always in the plural in the NT) is often rendered "pilgrims" or "sojourners" or "aliens" in English. It expresses the idea of one who is traveling away from home, whose present residence is only temporary. Thus the term is used in Hebrews 11:13 to refer to the OT patriarchs who, because they had not yet possessed their homeland, were wanderers on the earth. The notion of the Christian as pilgrim, when combined with other verses in Scripture (e.g., Eph. 2:6, 19; Phil. 3:20) which allude to our citizenship in heaven, is often thought to mean that the earth is not our home; that we are waiting for a better, heavenly reality which has nothing to do with this present world. Augustine coined the phrase *resident aliens* to describe the state of believers who currently find themselves living on the earth. To many Christians it seems foolhardy to invest significant effort in the

While the New Jerusalem is most likely only to serve as a pattern for our cultural efforts and will not be the result of man's efforts (being "a city whose architect and builder is God" [Heb. 11:10], having many mansions "prepared" for us by Jesus [John 14:2]), it still is a striking affirmation that our culutural efforts are not misguided or opposed to God's ideals. Yet one of the most striking things we read in John's description of the New Jerusalem at the end of Revelation 21 is this, which would appear to have astonishing implications on our understanding of the end of culutural history:

> [24]And the nations of those who are saved shall walk in its [the city's] light, and the kings of the earth bring their glory and honor into it.
>
> . . . .
>
> [26]And they shall bring the glory and honor of the nations into it.

These verses raise the following pressing question: What is it that is being brought into the New Jerusalem? What does the apostle mean by "glory and honor"?

The Greek words used here, *doxe* ("glory" in the NKJV; "splendor" in the NIV) and *time* ("honor") are used widely in the NT, especially in relationship to God. The use of the word *doxe* in secular Greek denotes the ideas of pomp and earthly majesty ascribed to objects based upon the opinions of others; the term was rarely used to describe personal character qualities as we commonly use the word in English today (i.e., "honorable"). As such, the term has a decidedly material, almost visual character. (It was not until the writing of the Septuagint that the term took on an additional meaning of a personal luminous manifestation, as it is used of God's *shekinah* or *kabod*.) Very often the Bible uses *doxe* to refer to actual physical objects of high value or beauty. For example, Jesus was tempted by the devil with "all the kingdoms of the world and their glory" (Matt. 4:8; cf. Matt. 6:29; LXX of 1 Chr. 29:25; Esther 1:4; Is. 16:14; 35:2; 60:13). It would seem that that is the likely use of the term in Revelation 21:24 and 26, although many would dispute this (see following discussion). The word *time* is used to describe something bearing esteem, worth, or value and thus refers to actual material objects of high worth (cf. 1 Tim. 5:17). The idea that verses 24 and 26 describe the importation of actual valuable goods into the holy city does not seem to contradict the meaning of *doxe* and *time*. These glorious and honorable goods, being *"of"* the kings of the earth and the nations, must be describing objects of human manufacture—*culturative* stuff.

Anthony Hoekema, in *The Bible and the Future*, proposes that we accept just such a conclusion:

> One could say that according to these words, the inhabitants of the earth will include people who attained great prominence and exercised great power on the present earth—kings, leaders and the like. One could also say that whatever people have done on this earth which glorified God will be remembered in the life to come (see Rev. 14: 13). But more must be said. Is it too much to say that, according to these verses, the cultural development of the earth if we do not, in fact, belong here.

But the scripture passages are plentiful which teach that the earth—albeit renewed and glorified—will be our new home (Is. 60; 65:17ff; Matt. 5:5; Rom. 8:21; 2 Pet. 3:13; Rev. 21–22); that we are destined to continue to have a physical existence in glorified bodies (1 Cor. 15:35ff; Phil. 3:21); and that we will continue to rule the New Earth (Rev. 22:5) and serve God (Rev. 7:15) as we did in Eden (for more on this see the postscript following this chapter). If this present earth is indeed our eventual home, as it was for Adam, why did the apostle Peter call his readers aliens? One possible reason why the saints in Asia Minor were called aliens was the hostile, pagan culture which was a constant threat to the churches in this region. (It was here that Roman persecution was often most severe.) As the Church was to prosper in later times, gaining the upper hand as it did, for example, in Reformation countries, the label "pilgrim" would have lost much of its resonance for contemporary readers. Nevertheless, it is true that Christians of any era must face the continuing existence of evil and the effects of sin in society. In this sense we are alienated from all that is ungodly in this present world.

I would suggest that Augustine had it backwards: that we are not "resident aliens" but *alienated residents*. We are grieved at the present state of affairs on our beloved earth and long and pray for its liberation from the curse and sin (Rom. 8:19ff; Luke 11:2). Our situation can be compared to a prince who is living *in cognito* in a rebel province belonging to his father, the king. This territory will one day be rightfully his, but right now the prince risks great harm from his insurgent neighbors if his true identity were ever to be revealed. Thus this prince would be an alien in his own country. We Christians find ourselves in a similar situation. As heirs of the promised inheritance (Gal. 3:27; Eph. 1:11, 6:3), we find ourselves in a world full of evil, sin, and misery. But we live with the hope that the rebels will be forcibly removed from the

unique contributions of each nation to the life of the present earth will enrich the life of the new earth? Shall we then perhaps inherit the best products of culture and art which this earth has produced?

Hoekema points us to the words of Revelation 14:13: "'Blessed are the dead who die in the Lord from now on.' 'Yes,' says the Spirit, 'that they may rest from their labors, and their works [*erga*] follow them.'" Here we see the *works* for which man was created (Gen. 2:15) and later redeemed (Eph. 2:10) apparently being taken up into eternity! Whatever these goods that will be brought into heaven are, we know that they must be holy, because John says in Revelation 21:27, "There shall by no means enter it anything that defiles or causes an abomination or a lie."

The likelihood that John is describing an ingathering of actual physical artifacts made in previous human history is enhanced by the vision of the new "City of the LORD"/ "Zion" (v. 14) foretold in Isaiah 60, which has so many striking parallels with Revelation 21 and 22. This has led many commentators to conclude that the two visions describe the same future reality. Both are cities whose gates are never shut (Is. 60:11; Rev. 21:25), both have God as the light source (Is. 60:19–20; Rev. 21:23), both celebrate the total absence of human suffering (Is. 60:18; Rev. 21:4), both feature the nations standing in God's divine light (Is. 60:1–3; Rev. 21:24), and both feature a magnificent ingathering of goods from the nations of the earth. Isaiah tells us the treasures that will be ushered into Zion will include gold, silver, and other precious materials (vs. 6, 9, 17), livestock and camels (vs. 6–7), extravagant building materials (v. 13), etc. This will be "glory and honor" indeed!

This has by no means been the prominent view of Revelation 21:24 and 26. Most commentators have concluded that this view of the "glory and honor" to be brought into the New Jerusalem cannot be squared with other NT passages (e.g., 2 Pet. 3:10–11; Heb. 12:26-29) that seem to describe the total destruction of this present earth and its contents. The common sentiment is, "It's all going to burn!" After all, did not Jesus say, "Heaven and earth will pass away . . ." (Matt. 24:35)? Upon closer examination, I believe that these passages do not necessarily conflict with a view of "glory and honor" referring to actual man-made works from this present age that will be part of the furnishings of the future city of God.

We examine Hebrews 12:26–29 first. Earlier in the chapter the writer to the Hebrews indicates that he is speaking of a future Mount Zion—the "heavenly Jerusalem" (v. 22). Then, in verses 26–27 he states,

> [26]But now He has promised, saying "Yet once more I shake not only the earth, but also heaven." [27]Now this, "Yet once more," indicates the removal of those things that are being shaken, as of things that are made, that the things which cannot be shaken may remain.

The key question raised by this passage is what is meant by those "things" that are removed because they are being shaken by God. These things are described as having earth (Matt. 13:41), and once it is renewed and refurnished, we will be returned to our home to live for ever and ever in God's glorious presence.

been "made" (often translated "created") and thus appear to be actual objects. (It should be noted that many commentators view the "things" shaken and removed to be the "things" associated with the obsolete Levitical priesthood discussed in the earlier chapters of the book. Thus this passage would have no direct bearing on the interpretation of Revelation 21.) Does this include *every* object—*all* "made" things which are to be found in the creation? Is everything to be shaken and removed? The text clearly indicates this is not the case. There will be "things" which cannot be shaken and thus will remain (v. 27). Clearly these "things" too must have been part of creation, since there are no "things" which exist which were not created by God! (Rev. 4:11). The argument put forth in Hebrews 12:25–29 ends with the words, "For our God is a consuming fire." This would seem to link the idea of the final removal of impermanent objects by a divine "shaking" with the burning foretold in 2 Peter 3:10–13.

We quote this challenging passage at length:

> [10]But the day of the Lord will come as a thief in the night, in which the heavens will pass away with a great noise, and the elements will melt with fervent heat; both the earth and the works [*erga*] that are in it will be burned up. [11]Therefore, since these things will be dissolved, what manner of persons ought you to be in holy conduct and godliness, [12]looking for and hastening the coming of the day of God, because of which the heavens will be dissolved, being on fire, and the elements will melt with fervent heat? [13]Nevertheless we, according to His promise, look for the new heavens and a new earth in which righteousness dwells.

In this passage, Peter describes what will happen to the heavens and the earth, and the "elements" and "works" found therein: these are "to pass away with a great noise [*rhoizedon*]", they will "melt" and "dissolve" under great heat, and the works (presumably of men) in particular will be "burned up." At first reading, this passage might well be taken to mean that there will be nothing of this present earth and its contents remaining after the Second Coming of Christ and the Last Judgment. If all the works are to be "burned up," it will be very difficult for there to be works that can follow the saints into heaven (Rev. 14:13). It should be pointed out that a large number of Greek manuscripts have the word for "laid bare" instead of "burned up" in verse 10. Thus

Peter would be speaking of an ethical evaluation of these works in judgment rather than their destruction. But even if we are to accept the reading "burned up," this does not necessarily imply that all of the works will be totally destroyed.

A possible reconciliation of 2 Peter 3 and Revelation 21 (and even Hebrews 12!) is to be found in Exodus 40:34–38 (cf. 1 Kgs. 8:10–11):

> [34]Then the cloud covered the tabernacle of meeting, and the glory of the LORD filled the tabernacle. [35]And Moses was not able to enter the tabernacle of meeting, because the cloud rested above it, and the glory of the LORD filled the tabernacle. . . . [38]For the cloud of the LORD was above the tabernacle by day, and the fire was over it by night, in the sight of all of the house of Israel, throughout all their journeys.

The glory of the LORD manifested itself to the OT Jews alternatively by a cloud and by fire (cf. Ex. 14:24). This was how the Israelites knew God to be a "consuming fire" (Ex. 24:17; Deut. 4:24; Ps. 18:8; Is. 30:27, 30). What is remarkable about the passage in Exodus 40 is that the LORD's cloud/fire falls upon the newly completed and dedicated tabernacle, and it is *not* consumed! In grace, the divine fire does not destroy the tabernacle and its furnishings but refines it—purges out every vestige of sin and impurity—so that it is suitably prepared to be in God's holy presence (cf. Mal. 3:2–3; 1 Cor. 3:13–15). In the case of the tabernacle (and the temple—1 Kgs. 8:10–11), the cultural works of mortal men are not necessarily destroyed by God's fiery presence. God's grace may extend to the perfecting of man's *works* just as His grace may sanctify the human *person*. To return to 2 Peter 3:10ff, the apostle seems to give us a picture of a "roaring" wild fire (*rhoizedon* is a very colorful word evoking the sound of something whooshing through the air) spreading across the whole face of the earth. We may speak colloquially of a wild fire "burning up" a forest to mean a destruction of the underbrush and small growth, allowing the mature trees to remain and flourish. It seems highly plausible that the burning up of the "works" in verse 10 can refer similarly to the destruction of the majority of unworthy, unredeemable works so thoroughly pervaded by sin's effects that God's fire of refinement leaves nothing behind to take into heaven (cf. Matt. 13:41–42). Those works found to have some real substance after being tested by fire will indeed follow the saints into the New Jerusalem (Rev. 14:13). Thus we may conclude that God's glorious creation and the fullness thereof will not be *euthanized* at the end of history but will be graciously restored and renewed (Rom. 8:21).

It should additionally be noted that the Greek word used for "new" in Revelation 21:1–2 and 2 Peter 3:13 is not *neos* but *kainos*. The choice of words here by John and Peter is very important. The word *neos* means new in time or origin (i.e., "brand new"), while the word *kainos* means new in nature or quality. Thus it may be concluded that the "new heaven(s) and New Earth" describes not the appearance of a universe totally other than the present one but a universe that has been divinely renewed and stands in real continuity with the present heaven and earth.

Revelation 21:26 appears to teach us that we are not merely to perform the work God has prepared for us beforehand to do (Eph. 2:10). Some of our works will actually follow us into heaven (Rev. 14:13) and furnish the New Jerusalem. If this is indeed the biblical teaching on the destiny of human works, then this has major implications on our understanding of our culturative calling before God. Rather than seeing human culturative endeavors as "polishing brass on a sinking ship," as many contemporary evangelical Christians conclude on the basis of their pessimistic view of 2 Peter 3:10 (the total destruction of all of man's works), we conclude that there will be a real continuity between this world and the next, between the works done now to the glory of God and the furnishings we will find in the next life. This gives Christians a profound hope and motivation for doing culture *now*. While it could be argued that doing culture "unto the Lord" should be motivation enough, until we grasp the biblical teaching that our culturative works will in fact have *eternal* significance, our works will always be undervalued and ignored in favor of more "spiritual" projects. It is only in believing along with Scripture that the best of our art works and our mathematical proofs and our poetry and our scholarly theories will actually contribute to the glory of the life to come that we will loose ourselves from the shallowness and triviality that marks so much of present-day Christendom and strive to take our culturative calling seriously with all worship and joy. As G. B. Caird said in his commentary on Revelation 21:

> Nothing from the old order which has value in the sight of God is disbarred from entry into the new. John's heaven is no world-denying Nirvana, into which men may escape from the incurable ills of sublunary existence, but the seal of affirmation on the goodness of God's creation. The treasure that men find laid up in heaven turns out to be the treasures and wealth of the nations, the best they have known and loved on earth redeemed of all imperfections and transfigured by the radiance of God.

POSTSCRIPT:

CULTURE AND SABBATH

To summarize what has been said in the earlier sections of this book: culture is the divine calling of mankind to transform the earth from its initial, natural state to a glorious network of gardens and cities spread out across the whole face of the globe. Our "cultural mandate" is grounded in God's command for us to rule the earth (Gen. 1:28) and work the ground (with which we share our substance and namesake), bringing out the hidden potentialities lying within (Gen. 2:15). We have seen that this calling to make culture (which was inaugurated *before* the Fall) was never rescinded but was boldly reiterated in the NT commandment to work to the glory of God (Eph. 2:10). Moreover, the works of man will find a place in the New Earth, albeit refined and sanctified by God's righteous fire (Rev. 14:13). Culture has a prominent role in God's program for the earth and for the human race, having been woven into the whole tapestry of mankind's history from the very beginning to the consummation . . . and beyond.

A correct understanding of work (*abad* in Genesis 2) is crucial for a biblical view of culture. We saw in detail how the Hebrew verb has the threefold connotation of work, service, and worship. Thus we see that the human race is called to interact deliberately with the earth—*work*, till, cultivate—while at the same time lovingly *serving* his divine Master with undivided devotion and *worshiping* his Maker. Culture is never to be an autonomous gesture on the part of mankind but is instead to be undertaken in humble submission to God's law-command. In the making of culture, work and worship are inseparable. Culture was meant to be done to the glory of God (1 Cor. 10:31).

The OT understanding of work and its place within the life of faith and culture comes into bold relief in the biblical command to keep the sabbath. The sabbath command is found in the very heart of the Mosaic covenant the LORD established with his people at Sinai—the Ten Commandments:

> Remember the Sabbath day, to keep it holy. Six days you shall labor [abad] and do all your work [melakah], but the seventh day is the Sabbath of the LORD your God. In it you shall do no work [melakah]: you, nor your son, nor your daughter, nor your male servant, nor your female servant, nor your cattle, nor the stranger who is within your gates. (Ex. 20:8–10)

Work and sabbath are not presented as opposites in the Scriptures; rather they complement one another. For six days of the week humankind is to do all its work—the raising of families and the building of culture. This is to be done in the spirit of worship (a core meaning of abad), glorifying God. The seventh day is to be a ceasing (the root meaning of the Hebrew word sabbath) from "everyday" work (important as it is!) so that God's people may focus upon the sacred work of worship. The day is to be hallowed—set apart. It is to be significantly different from the other days of the week.

Upon close analysis, it becomes clear that sabbath keeping is not only contrasted with work in general but with the particular work associated with the making of culture. In Exodus 34:21 God commands, "Six days you shall work [abad], but on the seventh day you shall rest; in plowing time and in harvest you shall rest." Here, at the two most critical junctures of a crop-based agriculture, mankind is reminded that he must still rest on the sabbath, even when the temptation to work is very strong. Genesis 2:15 established farming as the most basic culturative endeavor. By extension we may conclude that this verse implies that there are bounds to man's vocation to make culture, one of the most important of which is keeping the sabbath day holy. This culture/sabbath contrast is also revealed in two other passages in Exodus (Ex. 31:12–17; 35:1–3), which also prescribe the death penalty for those who would profane that which the

LORD has declared holy. Both passages appear next to extensive passages describing the elaborate construction and preparation of the tabernacle (Ex. 25:1–31:11; 35:4–39:43). This is not a coincidence. This juxtaposition clearly was meant to warn the Israelite artisans that even in the building of the tabernacle and its furnishings—as vitally important as these were for worship and God's purposes in redemptive history—the sabbath was still to be observed. As was discussed in part 1 of this book, the building of the tabernacle and, later, the Temple were both paradigms on a small scale (microcosms) of mankind's comprehensive, global culturative task. As basic and inescapable as our culturative calling is (and as holy and high a calling as building the tabernacle was in Moses' day), we must always be willing to submit ourselves to the Word of God and its prescriptions.

Culture is a basic part of the regular weekly cycle of work and rest/worship, culture and cultus. It is part of the steady rhythm of life God's people are now meant to embrace and enjoy. The sabbath reminds us on a continuing basis that culture is part of God's time and God's history. Since God is sovereign over time and history, our culture-making is not in vain (Ps. 90:17).

CREATION, REDEMPTION & CONSUMMATION

We can say more about the theological significance of the sabbath and the light it sheds on a biblical understanding of work and culture-making. The Scriptures teach us that the sabbath is closely related to the three major historical motifs of creation, redemption, and the consummation of all things at the end of this present age. The sabbath was to be a perpetual ordinance for the covenant community (Ex. 31:13, 16), observed throughout all history because it is related to the totality of history. In observing how the doctrine of the sabbath relates to these three critical divine epochs, we will gain deeper insight into the meaning of human work and culture.

Creation. In the first account of the Ten Commandments in Exodus 20, the meaning/rationale of the fourth commandment (quoted previously) is revealed in verse 11: "For in six days the LORD made the heavens and the earth, the sea, and all that is in

them, and rested the seventh day. Therefore the LORD blessed
the Sabbath day and hallowed it" (cf. Ex. 31:17). This hearkens
the reader back to the creation account and opening words of
Genesis 2:

> And on the seventh day God ended His work [*melakah*] which He
> had done and He rested on the seventh day from all His work
> [*melakah*] which He had done. Then He blessed the seventh day
> and sanctified it, because in it He rested from all the work
> [*melakah*] which God had created and made. (Gen. 2:2–3)

While the word *sabbath* does not appear in Genesis 2, God's *resting* from the work of forming and furnishing the heavens and
earth (Gen. 1), and His *blessing* and *hallowing* (sanctifying) of the
seventh day are clearly in view in Exodus 20:11. Most scholars
agree that the Hebrew word meaning *to rest* or *to cease* (*shabat*,
note how the term is used in Gen. 8:22) is etymologically related
to the term sabbath. God's people are to rest on the sabbath
(Ex. 31:15) and cease from their everyday culturative work just
as God rested from His creational work. But the Scriptures also
teach that this ceasing is not absolute. The sabbath is not to be a
day of inactivity and lethargy. God continues to work in His acts
of providence and redemption, though He has ceased His
creational work (John 5:17). His people also are to "work" on
this day—following Christ's example—in acts of worship, healing, and service (WCF chap. 21.8).

Though the Scriptures make an important distinction between
God's creating (*bara* in the Hebrew, used exclusively of God)
and mankind's working and making, our sabbath-keeping clearly
relates our cultural endeavors (work) with God's creational activities. Man's culture-making is analogous to God's world-
making. Genesis uses the striking term *melakah* (*work*, a more
generic synonym of *abad*) to describe God's activities in Genesis 1,
indicating the close relationship between our work and God's.
Work must be seen as a good thing (not the result of sin or the
curse) because God does it too! Both *melakah* and *abad* appear in
the fourth commandment (quoted on p. 96 with these words in
brackets), relating both ideas of work to the sabbath. The sabbath, in pointing us back to God's work in creation, is a continual
reminder that our earth-transformational work is of great value

and importance because it reflects the glorious activity of the Creator.

Redemption. The second recounting of the Ten Commandments in Deuteronomy 5 contains a different explanation of the meaning/rationale of the fourth commandment:

> That your male servant and your female servant may rest as well as you. And remember that you were a slave in the land of Egypt, and the LORD your God brought you out from there by a mighty hand and an outstretched arm; therefore the LORD your God commanded you to keep the Sabbath day. (Deut. 5:14–15)

Here we see that the sabbath is grounded in another mighty act of God: not creation (as in Exodus 20) but the exodus. The sabbath was to be a continual reminder to the OT people of God that it was the LORD who brought them out from under the cruel bondage of the Egyptians and liberated them by an astounding series of supernatural events so that they could be free to serve their God in the Land of Promise (which at the historical moment of Deuteronomy the Israelites were poised to inhabit). The exodus is a picture of what Christ was to accomplish through His sacrificial death and victorious resurrection. (This is why the sabbath is now celebrated on the first day of the week—the Lord's Day or Resurrection Day; see Acts 20:7; 1 Cor. 16:2.) The covenant people are to be liberated from the bondage and oppression of sin and Satan so that we may serve God as His bondservants (Luke 4:17–21; Rom. 6:15–22) in our cultural pursuits. As slaves of the Egyptians, the Hebrew people were unable to fulfill their calling to worship the LORD and build a culture to the glory of God. It was only through divine deliverance that they were brought to a place of rest (Deut. 12:10; Josh. 1:13; 21:43–45; 23:1). Having been freed from oppression and wandering, they were at liberty to serve God with their culturative and cultic pursuits. The sabbath also granted one day a week of freedom and rest to the slaves of society so that they could worship the LORD without the encumbrance of their duties to their masters. Thus the sabbath commandment points to a time in the future when all of God's sons and daughters will be entirely free from sin, toil, and misery. This eternal "rest" that we will enjoy on the New Earth will be explored in detail in the following section.

Just as the sabbath alludes to the doctrine of justification in picturing for us the freedom we have now gained from sin's oppression, our guilt, and God's wrath, so the sabbath pictures our sanctification as well:

> Surely My Sabbaths you shall keep, for it is a sign between Me and you and throughout all your generations, that you may know that I am the LORD who sanctifies you. You shall keep the Sabbath, therefore, for it is holy to you. (Ex. 31:13–14; cf. Ezek. 20:12)

It was the LORD who declared one day in seven to be holy, distinct from the other six days, set apart for divine service and sacred assembly (Lev. 23:3). The sanctity of the sabbath (reflected in keeping the day distinct from the other days of the week) regularly reminded the covenant people that it was God who *sanctified* them, removed from them the stain of sin, and set them apart for divine service. God sanctifies His people by the means of grace so that they may work once again (as in Eden) self-consciously to the glory of God. (Is this not the role of Scripture described in 2 Timothy 3:16–17?) The sabbath day is to be, for God's children, a necessary day of consecration so that the work we do the other six days of the week may be a pleasing aroma to the Lord.

Consummation. The sabbath is also a type of the future glory the people of God will enjoy on the New Earth, after the vestiges of sin are altogether removed from creation. Calvin put it this way:

> The Lord through the seventh day has sketched for his people the coming perfection of his Sabbath in the Last Day, to make them aspire to this perfection by unceasing meditation upon the Sabbath throughout life. (*Institutes*, 2.8.30)

The author of Hebrews puts the future significance of the sabbath into focus in chapter 4:

> [3]For we who have believed do enter that rest, as He has said: "So I swore in My wrath, 'They shall not enter my rest,'" although the works were finished from the foundation of the world. [4]For He has spoken in a certain place of the seventh day in this way: "And

God rested on the seventh day from all His works"; [5]and again in this place: "They shall not enter my rest."

[6]Since therefore it remains that some must enter it, and those to whom it was first preached did not enter it because of disobedience, [7]again He designates a certain day, saying in David, "Today," after such a long time, as it has been said: "Today, if you will hear His voice, do not harden your hearts." [8]For if Joshua had given them rest, then He would not afterward have spoken of another day. [9]There remains therefore a rest for the people of God. [10]For he who has entered this rest has himself also ceased from his works as God did from His.

Verse 8 makes it clear that the rest promised in Deuteronomy 12:10 and achieved by Joshua in the Promised Land (Josh. 21:44) was not the ultimate fulfillment of the sabbath in human history. Psalm 95 (quoted in this passage of Hebrews) states that there is another rest waiting for the people of God, for those who remain faithful to "God's voice." The Greek term for *rest* in verse 9 makes the relationship of this future rest and sabbath utterly clear: "There remains therefore a *rest* [*sabbatismos*, a "sabbath keeping" as suggested by F. F. Bruce] for the people of God." (The other occurrences of "rest" in this passage use the Greek word *katapausis*.)

What does the writer of Hebrews have in mind by this future "sabbath keeping"? Many commentators have suggested that the cessation from works mentioned in verse 10 describes the state of the believer under the principle of *sola fides*. Since we are "justified by faith," we are able to rest from our works as a (futile) means of meriting God's favor. While this idea may be partially in view, it cannot be the whole meaning of our "rest" in verses 9 and 10, since this rest is a future reality, something we have not yet entered ("There *remains* therefore a rest . . ."—see also verse 11). That the "sabbath keeping" mentioned in verse 9 is a picture of our future eternal state seems clear when we compare this passage to Revelation 14:13 (discussed at the end of part 2 in relation to the place that cultural works will have on the New Earth):

"Blessed are the dead who die in the Lord from now on."
"Yes," says the Spirit, "that they may rest from their labors, and their works follow them."

Those who have died "in the Lord" are brought to an eternal state of rest from their labors. The Greek word for "labors" here is key to understanding this verse. *Kopos* is a decidedly negative term, derived from the word for striking or beating (*kopos* is often translated as "trouble" in the NT). The saints will no longer be subject to the toil and drudgery of labor they experience in this life because of the curse following the Fall (Gen. 3:17–19). This verse does not teach that those who have entered the eternal state will no longer work in any sense. To return to the analogy used in Hebrews 4, we may conclude that our future "rest" will be like that which the Israelites experienced under the guidance of Joshua. God had given His people rest from Egyptian slavery, wandering in the wilderness, and their enemies in Canaan. But there was still work to be done. The Jews were to build a culture in line with the revelation they had received from the LORD. The apostle John tells us that God's people will, after death, once again rule over the earth (Rev. 22:5; 5:10) and that we will serve Him continually in His temple (i.e., the New Earth, the place where God dwells—Rev. 7:15). These twin ideas of rule and service (*abad*) take us back to the seminal commands of the cultural mandate in Genesis 1:26ff and 2:15. It seems likely that culture will continue on the New Earth as it does on the old— but without any hint of sin or toil. Lorraine Boettner in *Immortality* describes our future prospects in these terms:

> The intermediate state is a state of rest and happiness. That, however, does not mean that life there, or life in heaven, will be characterized by idleness and inactivity. Far from it. In the first place, "rest," in Scriptural language, carries with it the idea of *satisfaction in labor,* or *joy in accomplishment.* Even in this world we often find rest in a change in the kind of work we are doing. The activity of the saints is no longer "toil" or "labor," in the sense that it is irksome or tiresome. In this world man in his fallen condition is under sentence to earn his bread by the sweat of his face (Gen. 3:19). Much of his work is misdirected, monotonous, repetitious, and vain. But there all of the unpleasant features are removed and it is given a new direction, with new motives, and is a joy to perform. It is no longer directed primarily toward ourselves, nor toward any creature, but toward God. The heavenly life is one of uninterrupted progress, always upward and onward. The saints are "before the throne of God; and they serve him day and night in his temple," Revelation 7:15—they serve Him in work as well as in worship, His temple perhaps including the entire created universe.

WORK AND WORSHIP

The sabbath marks a basic chronological division in the life of the covenant community between work (including culture-making) and worship. For six days God's people are to do all their work (note that the biblical workweek was six days, not five), but on the seventh day (the remaining day of the week), they are to cease (rest) from their labors and devote their energies and attention to the formal worship of God. It is important to note that in this sacred division of time there was no sacred/secular distinction. One's everyday work was the LORD's work even though there is a differentiation made between it and the formal worship that was to be celebrated on the sabbath day. As we explained above, the work/worship distinction is not absolute. "Everyday" work is to be done as an act of worship (with a worshipful attitude) toward God, and formal, sabbath-day worship involves various kinds of work (prayer, singing, preaching, sacraments, etc.). For God's people, the sabbath is a holy day to be spent in reflection, preparation, and consecration so that the work done on the other six days will be honoring to the Lord.

One question that is often raised is whether there was sabbath observance in Eden before the Fall. I propose that before the fall of mankind into sin there was no sabbath-day distinction. For the original man and woman, every day was simultaneously a day of worship and a day of work; the work of culture-making was formal worship perfectly and transparently offered up to God. It should be pointed out right away that this is by no means the majority opinion among conservative, reformed scholars. Most have taught that the sabbath was formally instituted before the Fall. John Murray, for example, called the sabbath (along with marriage and labor) a "creation ordinance," arguing that

> This sequence of six days of labour and one of rest would have applied to Adam in the state of innocence and in a state of confirmed integrity in the event of successful probation; and the most reasonable supposition is that the revelation to Adam would have taken the form of the revelation we possess in Genesis 2:2, 3.... The argument commonly advanced is that the silence of Genesis on the matter of the sabbath indicates that there was no weekly sabbath in patriarchal times and that it was first instituted after the Exodus. Genesis 2:2, 3 proves that the sabbath is a creation

ordinance and, as such, must have been known to Adam and his contemporaries." *(Principles of Conduct*, p. 34)

(This view of the institution of the sabbath is also hinted at in WCF chap. 21.7, though not explicitly stated.) Does the teaching of God's resting in Genesis 2:2–3 imply that the sabbath must have been observed by man before the Fall?

John Murray concedes that the Scriptures are silent on this matter. While the opening chapters of Genesis clearly teach that before the entrance of sin into the world, marriage (Gen. 2:22) and work/culture-making (Gen. 1:26; 2:15) were actual historical realities instituted by God and undertaken by man, there is no indication that sabbath-keeping was commanded by God or observed by mankind. Even the grounding of the sabbath-day observance in God's pattern of six days of creation and one day of rest in Exodus 20:11 does not necessarily imply that sinless Adam observed a distinct sabbath. We should be careful therefore not to be too dogmatic on this issue either in favor of a pre-fall sabbath observance or an alternative view.

A view which favors the idea that a distinct sabbath day was not observed by man before the Fall has the advantage of emphasizing the strong parallel between Adam in Eden in his sinless estate and redeemed mankind on the New Earth in their state of everlasting sinless glory. In Eden and on the New Earth, the entirety of life would be sabbath and worship. This does not imply that work and culture are excluded; rather they are part of a work-worship unity. Without the detrimental effect of sin, work and worship would have been for mankind one and the same thing—*worship*. Man was created by God to glorify (worship) Him by exercising dominion of the earth and work/culture-making. "Workship" was to be the norm. After the Fall, mankind was in need of redemption and sanctification in order to be able to serve God as originally intended. The sabbath/workweek distinction became the vehicle whereby man could celebrate his need for liberation from sin and sanctification in order to be consecrated and equipped for divine service in work. When sin has been totally eradicated from soul and body, and we at last are glorified (Rom. 8:30), the elect will finally enjoy the eternal sabbath—a time of "workship" more glorious and splendid than that of Eden.

History can then be seen to have a God-directed symmetry

centered around the crucifixion and resurrection of Christ as follows:

Paradise	Workdays–Sabbath	*Christ*	Sabbath–Workdays	New Earth
work-worship	OT weekly pattern	Jubilee	NT weekly pattern	work-worship
unity	creation orientation		future orientation	unity

The Lord Jesus Christ is the center of history. His death and resurrection achieved an entirely new order both in the administration of the covenant of grace (the requirements of the ceremonial law having been fulfilled in Him) and in our orientation toward time and history. Before Christ, the sabbath day was on the last day of the week. The OT sabbath was a day of completion and a culmination of the workweek which had gone on before. After Christ, the sabbath day was shifted to the first day of the week (resurrection day). Thus the NT sabbath became a day of commissioning and a commencement of the workweek to come. In the OT order of the workweek *followed by* the sabbath, the historical orientation was primarily directed back to Eden as a norm, with an eye toward the future and the coming city "whose builder and maker is God" (Heb. 11:10, cf. 11:16; the OT saints had only a shadowy understanding of the glorious future which has been more fully revealed to us in the NT). In the NT order of the workweek *following* the sabbath, the historical orientation is primarily directed forward to the New Jerusalem as an exemplary goal, with an eye to the norms of Eden. In between the OT and NT orders stands Jesus Christ, who through his efficacious sacrifice and victorious resurrection achieved the ultimate Jubilee.

The OT covenant community not only observed the weekly sabbath and the annual festival days (which were also days where work was to cease), but also sabbath years (Lev. 25:1–7), when the land was given time to rest. At the culmination of seven sabbath year–cycles, there was an extra sabbath year (a *double sabbath*) on the fiftieth year called the year of Jubilee (Lev. 25:8–55). In the Jubilee year, not only was the land to have an extra year of rest, but agricultural property was to be returned to the original owner-families, and slaves were to be set free. The fifty-year cycle of the Jubilee created a shift in the counting of the seven-year pattern. For example, assuming the first year as year "1," the sabbath years would follow this series:

7 – 14 – 21 – 28 – 35 – 42 – 49, 50 [the Jubilee] – 57 – 64 – 71 – 78, etc.

The sabbath years following the Jubilee (fiftieth) year would no longer fall on a multiple of seven (i.e., 56. . .63 . . .70, etc.). Thus the shift in the yearly cycle helped symbolize the remarkable societal transposition—the restoration of land ownership and the liberation of slaves—ushered in by the Jubilee.

The resurrection of Christ marked another double sabbath event with cosmic (not just societal) ramifications. Jesus rose on the first day of the week (Matt. 28:1). Thus the first "resurrection day"—the inauguration of the NT sabbath—succeeded the last day of the previous week—the OT sabbath day. This *double sabbath of days* (not years) signaled that the death and resurrection of Christ was a Jubilee far more grand and comprehensive than the Jubilee under the Mosaic system. The death and resurrection of Jesus Christ signified a new world order where the sons and daughters of God were decisively liberated from their slavery to sin and the devil; the whole earth (not just land parcels in the territory of Israel) was returned to its rightful Owner to be given over as plunder to the elect (Eph. 4:8). The glorified, resurrected body and soul of our Lord is the firstfruits of the New Creation (1 Cor. 15:20ff) which He now labors through His Spirit to establish in history (John 14:1–3; Acts 1:1). The whole order of life on the planet Earth is forever changed. Time is changed. The way we order our week is changed. Jesus Christ has changed everything! But there is still work. There is still culture building. And there is still worship. The workweek/sabbath cycle continues on (albeit changed), sustained by the providential hand of God. And we wait—with groanings too deep for words—for the resurrection of our own bodies (Rom. 8), so that we can enter into our eternal state of glorious, blissful "workship" forevermore.

THE COMMON AND THE SACRED

The sabbath does not only lead the child of God to reflect upon the meaning, divine origin, and glorious destiny of work and worship, but it is also a constant reminder of the crucial division of beings and things into the categories of common, sacred, and profane. The sabbath was a *holy* day: "Remember the sabbath day to keep it holy" (Ex. 20:9). It was to be marked off as distinct—separate—from the other "common" days of the week. We have already noted how keeping the sabbath day holy was closely related to God's sanctifying activity with His people (Ex. 31:13; Ezek. 20:12). The LORD is a holy God. This is the ongoing proclamation of the angelic beings in heaven as they worship the King of kings on His throne (Is. 6:3; Rev. 4:8). Because God is holy, everything associated with Him must be holy. Hence we are confronted repeatedly with the scriptural command, "Be holy, for I am holy" (1 Pet. 1:16; cf. Lev. 11:44–45; 19:2; Deut. 7:6; 14:2; 28:9; Heb. 12:14).

The OT covenant community needed to be constantly vigilant in these matters. Failure to recognize what was holy and what was common could bring dire consequences. For example, Aaron was warned, "Do not drink wine or other intoxicating drink, you, nor your sons with you, when you go into the tabernacle of meeting, lest you die. It shall be a statute forever throughout all your generations, that you may distinguish between the holy and unholy, and between clean and unclean . . ." (Lev. 10:8–10; note: the term "unholy" here is better rendered "common"; cf. NIV and see following discussion). This command came after Aaron's sons Nadab and Abihu had been killed by the LORD for offering "profane" (or "strange") fire to Him in the tabernacle (vv. 1–2). The entire sacrificial system with its distinct community of priests and elaborate preparatory rituals, the prescribed washings and warnings against ceremonial defilement, the dietary laws and laws against mixing seed and cloth fibers—all these were constant reminders of the need for holiness and Israel's status as a *distinct* nation belonging to a holy God.

Even the structure of the temple complex reflected the distinct strata of OT society with its varying degrees of ceremonial holiness. As Alfred Edersheim explains in detail, the temple could be divided into at least seven zones of increasing exclusion and holiness. This included (in order of increasing holiness) the Court of the Gentiles (an enclosure for all people—Jew and non-Jew alike), the Women's Court (for Jews only—both men and women), the Men's Court (for Jewish men), the Levites' Court (for male descendants of the tribe of Levi), the Priest's Court (for the male descendants of Aaron and the temple attendants), and inside the temple proper, the Holy Place (for the priests only), and finally, the Most Holy Place (or the Holy of Holies). The Most Holy Place—the innermost zone in the temple complex—was where God dwelt between the cherubim atop the ark of the covenant (Ps. 90:1). This place was so holy that only one individual—the high priest—was ever allowed to enter it (and this only once a year on the Day of Atonement). The temple complex along with the rest of the Mosaic law—including the sabbath—pointed to the need for God's people to live and shape their lives in terms of holiness, because their God was a holy God.

The fact that believers are called to keep the sabbath day holy implies that the sabbath can be profaned:

> You shall keep the sabbath, therefore, for it is holy to you. Everyone who profanes it shall surely be put to death; for whoever does any work on it, that person shall be cut off from among his people. (Ex. 31:14)

The Bible places people and things into three distinct classes: holy, profane, and common. Those things which have been set apart by God (usually for service) are holy. They are to be treated differently than common or profane objects and can, if misused or debased, become tainted or ruined and no longer be of use in worship. Or they can become the object of God's holy wrath. The word translated "profane" in Exodus 31:14 is *halal*. It is most often translated "profane" or "defiled." The word is clearly an opposite to "holy" and is used for those who would break God's law (Zeph. 3:4; Ps. 89:31) or covenant (Ps. 55:20), as well as for those who would break the sabbath. A closely related Hebrew term is *hanep*, which refers to those things which are polluted and therefore unholy (Num. 35:33; Is. 24:5; Jer. 23:11). The adjectives *halal* and *hanep* are decidedly negative terms. Such things were to be avoided and without ceremonial cleansing were unholy and unfit for worship.

A close derivative of *halal* is *hol*, which is a more neutral term, that is, more akin to our word *common*—"And the priest answered David and said, 'There is no common bread on hand; but there is holy bread'" (1 Sam. 21:4). "Common" bread was not evil in and of itself; it was merely bread that had not been set apart for use in the tabernacle. Common bread was not ordinarily polluted, and eating it would not defile the one who ate it. Nevertheless, the holy showbread was distinct from common bread. Common things are non-holy rather than unholy. *Hol* is also used in Leviticus 10:10, which was quoted earlier: the priests must be able to distinguish between the holy and the common. Similarly, a distinction was to be drawn between the sabbath day and the other days of the week. The sabbath was holy while the other days were common. This does not make the other days (and the cultural work done on them) evil or unholy. Rather, they are to be considered apart from the formal worship which characterizes the sabbath day. Work/culture-making and formal worship were to be distinguished from one another until the consummation and the reestablishment of "workship" on the New Earth.

The NT post-resurrection era brought a new perspective on the issue of holy versus common. The book of Acts documents the transition. Many of the boundaries between holy and unholy, clean and unclean, were erased. Peter was the first to be confronted with this new order. After being presented with a vision of all sorts of animals, Peter was commanded to "kill and eat." Note the apostle's response:

> But Peter said, "Not so Lord! For I have never eaten anything common or unclean." And a voice spoke to him again the second time, "What God has cleansed you must not call common." (Acts 10:13–15)

God used this vision to prepare Peter for the inclusion of gentiles (unholy people) into the covenant community, beginning with Cornelius and his household. Gentiles could be included apart from the elaborate ceremonial washings and circumcision which proselytes to the Jewish religion usually underwent. This was a hard change to accept for many of the Jewish believers who had been diligently trained in the holy/unholy distinction. (Even Peter had his problems with this—see Gal. 2:11ff.) The message of Acts and the rest of the NT is that the Spirit of God is being poured out on "all flesh" (Acts 2:17). The barrier of hostility had been lifted between Jew and Gentile (Eph. 2:14f), and now in Christ "there is neither Greek or Jew, circumcised or uncircumcised, barbarian, Scythian, slave nor free, but Christ is all and in

all" (Col. 3:11; cf. Gal. 3:28). The ceremonial law had been fulfilled in Christ, and the distinctions that were a vital part of the
ceremonial law no longer had to be observed by believers. Nevertheless, the moral law was still in effect for the NT covenant
community, not as means of justification but as a tool for sanctification. Holiness is still a necessity for the people of God
(1 Pet. 1:15; Heb. 12:14), but it is no longer a matter of physical
defilement and ritual distinctions but a matter of the heart and
one's obedience to the commandments of God (Ps. 51:16–17;
John 14:15).

Jesus Christ is at the heart of this transition. The most profound declaration that there was a new understanding of the meaning of the holy and the common occurred at the time of Christ's
death: "And Jesus cried out with a loud voice, and yielded up His
spirit. Then, behold, the veil of the temple was torn in two from
top to bottom" (Matt. 27:50–51). The veil, which separated the
Most Holy Place from Holy Place and the rest of the temple
complex (and indeed from the rest of Israel and the whole earth)
was breached. The all-important distinction between the Holy of
Holies and all else was abrogated by a miracle of God. Theologians have often explained the significance of this event in terms
of God opening up access to Himself by the sacrifice of Christ
(Heb. 10:20) and indicating to us unambiguously that the OT
sacrificial system is now obsolete. Though these two explana-
tions of the meaning of the rending of the Temple veil are undoubtedly correct, I would propose that there is a third theological
principle which the tearing of the veil reveals to us. The removal
of the distinction between the Most Holy Place and the rest of
creation signals a time in history when the distinction between
heaven and earth shall be removed. The Most Holy Place was a
representation of God's throne room in heaven (cf. Is. 6:1ff).
The opening up of the veil does not only make a new way for the
believer to gain direct access to God, but it also opens up the way
for heaven—the place of absolute perfect holiness—to be joined
to the earth and its contents, including the refined cultural products of mankind (Rev. 21:24, 26).

The last prophetic vision recorded in the book of the prophet
Zechariah alludes to this amazing transformation. Consider these
astonishing words against the ceremonial backdrop of the OT

and its constant attention to the distinction between holy and common:

> In that day "HOLINESS TO THE LORD" shall be engraved on the bells of the horses. The pots in the LORD's house shall be like the bowls on the altar. Yes, every pot in Jerusalem and Judah shall be holiness to the LORD of hosts. Everyone who sacrifices shall come and take them and cook in them. In that day there shall no longer be a Canaanite in the house of the LORD of hosts. (Zech. 14:20–21; cf. Joel 3:17–18; Rev. 21:26–22:2)

The inscription "HOLINESS TO THE LORD" is found in only one other place in Scripture: on the plate of gold worn on the front of the headdress of the high priest as a part of his liturgical uniform—"So it shall be on Aaron's forehead, that Aaron may bear the iniquity of the holy things which the children of Israel hallow in all their holy gifts; and it shall always be on his forehead, that they may be accepted before the LORD" (Ex. 28:38). Thus this inscription was worn by the high priest when he entered the Most Holy Place on the Day of Atonement. In Zechariah's vision, this inscription, which previously had been associated with the epitome of holiness in the OT religious economy, is found on the most common, everyday cultural objects: horses' bells and cooking pots! Zechariah gives us a vision of a world where all of culture—even the mundane—is not common (non-holy) but holy, like the priest's vestments and the articles of the temple. That Zechariah is giving us a vision of the world to come is alluded to by the absence of the Canaanites (a group decidedly *unholy* in the OT worldview) from the scene. This parallels John's vision of the New Jerusalem not having anything in it that defiles (Rev. 21:27; cf. Joel 3:17).

The sabbath as a holy day (along with the OT ceremonial law and our present-day ongoing sanctification) points to a time in the future when the redeemed people of God (now glorified) and the whole earth in its glorious, renewed state will be set apart and made holy by God to be in His direct presence forever and ever (Rev. 22:5). There will be no hint of a sacred/secular distinction on the New Earth. The common (including cultural works done unto the Lord) will be consecrated and taken into the holy, and all that is profane will be utterly banished (Rev. 21:27). The sabbath day gives us hope that one day we will enter our eternal rest (Rev. 14:13), our sin will finally be purged from us, body and soul, and our work will be wholly consecrated and once again made to be perfect worship offered to our God. Our calling to rule the earth under and for God will be ultimately realized (1 Cor. 15:24–28; Heb. 2:8–9), and a robust culture full of truth and beauty and grace and holiness will abound across the face of the New Earth. Our call to transform the earth with culture will be realized at last to the everlasting praise of our Maker and Redeemer.

Soli Deo Gloria

APPENDIX:

TOWARD A CHRISTIAN VISION IN THE ARTS

The idea of taking from the world to benefit the causes of the Kingdom of God is often referred to as plundering. The plunder principle, as I will call it, takes its name from the exodus account, when God, "with a mighty hand and an outstretched arm" liberated the Jews from the captivity of the Egyptians. In the course of this miraculous event, God caused the Egyptians to hand over their gold and silver and other valuables to the Israelites, to their material and cultural benefit (Ex. 11:1–3; 12:35–36). In much the same way, Christians can take the best that the non-Christian world has to offer, plundering the aesthetic, intellectual, scientific, and technological treasure troves that God, by His providence and grace, has raised up for our cultural good.

But plunderer beware! We must not take from the world's cultural offerings indiscriminately. We must realize what we are dealing with. The gold that was given by God to the Israelites from the Egyptians was, undoubtedly, the very same gold with which they made the infamous golden calf. Likewise, before entering the Promised Land, the Jews were warned to have nothing to do with the idols of the nations living there. Not everything that God allowed to prosper in Canaan was for Israel's good. The same is true for us. The potential cultural treasures God places before us are there both to bless us as well as to test and to prove our obedience to Him.

By way of explanation, I want to state that not all products of human beings have the same degree of ethical depth; ice cream, for instance, is very different from art in this regard. This is not to say that ice cream has no ethical dimension; it's a matter of degree. Artworks, because they bear a greater involvement with their human maker, tend to reflect more of the character of their maker. We say, in common parlance, that the artist puts a lot of himself into his work. Consider God and His creation. We can rightly say that all of creation is personal because the world reflects attributes of its Maker. Likewise, when artworks are made by sinners (pre-glorified Christians included), the artworks necessarily reflect, proportionately, the sinfulness of each maker.

Any comprehensive Christian vision of the arts will contain a critical framework or strategy by which the good aspects of non-Christian art can be discerned from the bad and thereby be appropriated for God's glory. I have isolated four aspects of such a framework.

The first two are foundational. They involve reclamation and must be in place before we can proceed further. First, we must know the Bible—know it in the deepest, most intimate sense. The values and ideas and definitions and categories of God's Holy Word must permeate the entire mind, bringing about its total transformation and renewal (Rom. 12:1). When this process has taken hold of the believer, the task of responsibly critiquing the artistic products of the world is less difficult.

Second, we must be filled with the Holy Spirit, by which I mean a continual spiritual alertness in the believer whereby we are made to conform to the will of God, as revealed in His Scriptures. This means being disciplined and self-controlled. It is the sense used in Ephesians 5:18: "Do not get drunk on wine, which leads to debauchery. Instead be filled with the Spirit."

This continual state that we are to strive for should not be confused with the other meaning of being filled with the Spirit, exemplified in the case of the artisan Bezalel in Exodus 34 and the powerful preaching of the apostles in Acts. This filling is a temporary and extraordinary work of God bestowed for a particular purpose. By being continually filled with the Holy Spirit, we are enabled to understand the Bible, apply it wisely to each situation, and battle the sin in our lives that confounds our critical faculties.

Having immersed ourselves in the vast riches of Scripture (a process which is never finished), and having yielded ourselves to the Holy Spirit's power to conform us to the image of Christ, we are prepared to confront non-Christian art. We now begin the critical or evaluative process.

Third, then, I suggest that we make two critical distinctions that should help us in the evaluation of non-Christian art. The first is part of a "divide and conquer" strategy. We must apply the distinction of form and content in our effort to analyze non-Christian art. Dealing with the form—the formal or stylistic aspects of an artwork or performance, apart from its content; the meaning or message expressed in it—will help to minimize the confusion that often occurs between these related, though distinct, dimensions of artworks. Quite often, form and content are at odds.

Consider the Broadway play *The Gospel of Colonnus.* Here the ancient play of Sophocles was given a new twist; the original plot was told using a Black Gospel idiom fitted into a Christian fall-death-resurrection matrix. Christians who saw the play and failed to consider the distinction between form and content might be easily fooled by the joyous Gospel music and the overt references to resurrection and redemption. Yet such a Christian would have been duped. The pagan underpinnings of the Greek original were still present in full force, and the hopeful references to forgiveness and life everlasting were sheer blasphemy, depicted apart from their biblical source.

By considering the form and content separately, it would have been easier to pick out the good and bad aspects inherent in the play. Ideally, of course, form and content in an artwork should work together in a kind of aesthetic symbiosis, one reinforcing and amplifying the other. It necessarily follows, then, that the yoking together of a Christian style with a non-Christian message, or vice versa, will create disunity in the artwork and confusion in the mind of the viewer.

It must be repeated again that neither the content nor the form of artworks is neutral. Religious-philosophical presuppositions lie behind the development of every particular style. The challenge is to discover the relationship between the two. The Christian should be wary of adopting a style uncritically, if adopting a style can be done; style would seem to flow naturally from a particular personality and be manifest in the artwork, as God's person is manifested in His creation.

The second distinction we should utilize is one made by the Christian philosopher Al Wolters in his book *Creation Regained*. He proposes the distinction of structure and direction. By "structure," Wolters means the original ordering and arrangement of the world before the Fall. With the introduction of sin into creation, the original "good" structure was distorted and warped, affecting the whole of the creation (Rom. 8:19–21). The distortion is not so severe, however, that the character of the original cannot be discerned or that the original structure is irretrievable.

This last point is crucial for us. The term "direction" for Wolters denotes the orientation of people, actions, institutions, and objects before and after the Fall. Before the Fall, creation was entirely good (Gen. 1:31), and everything in creation was thus oriented toward God in continual praise and adoration. The introduction of sin, however, brought an altogether different "direction," an orientation away from God, toward sin and Satan. Wolter's notion of "direction" is closely linked to the concept of the Antithesis: the idea that there are two groups of people in the world, two kingdoms, one under the lordship of God and the other under Satan's illegitimate dominion. There is an irreconcilable conflict—put there by God Himself— between everything Christian and non-Christian. There is no neutrality. You must take sides at all times in everything you do.

The distinction between structure and direction is a powerful tool in our dealings with the fallen world. It provides the framework by which we can discern the way in which actions, institutions, and objects are utilized in ways consonant with, or antithetical to, the glory and intentions of God. It is then left to us to begin the process of undoing or reorienting these objects, institutions, etc., that we find straying from God.

We should also seek to rediscover and recover the norms and laws—the "structure"—that originally governed the objects, actions, institutions, and people before the Fall. We do this so that we might conform the present sin-cursed world to its original, pre-fall state while taking into account the good aspects of progress. Where the laws or norms are revealed directly in Scripture, the rediscovery-recovery process is fairly simple. We assent to the Bible's teaching on these matters. It is more difficult, though, to recover actions, institutions, etc., which the Scriptures do not directly address. Here we must step slowly and carefully, start with proven biblical principles, and apply them to a given situation. A thorough knowledge of the whole Bible and fervent prayer are essential in this process.

Let us examine how structure and direction can be put to work in an artistic context by considering two cubistic paintings by Picasso: *The Aficionado* of 1912 [fig. 1] and the *Mandolin and Guitar* of 1924 [fig. 2]. The first thing we notice about these two paintings is that, while they are both considered "Cubist," their styles are markedly different. In the case of *The Aficionado*, the colors are suppressed—limited mainly to dull browns and greys—and the subject is fragmented into dozens of juxtaposed parts or facets which at first sight seem to be placed in random fashion. *Mandolin and Guitar* presents us with a different stylistic story: the colors here are brighter and more vibrant. And though it is clear that Picasso is taking great liberty with the way in which he treats his subject matter, utilizing quite freely the devices of distortion and a lively interplay of shapes, textures, and colors throughout the work, there is still an overall feeling of unity in the work that is altogether missing in *The Aficionado*. One is still aware that there are distinct objects being represented in some sort of pictorial space in the later painting, while in the earlier painting, one is not quite sure where the man's face ends and his jacket begins, how his hands are distinct from the newspaper he is reading, etc.

Perhaps a brief explanation of the theory and development of Cubism will help us sort out what is happening here. Cubism is in many respects the logical culmination of modern art's repudiation of and reaction to the tyranny of one-point perspective which had dominated painting from the early Renaissance to the middle of the nineteenth century. Perspective was one way of solving the problem of depicting the three dimensions of the real world within the two dimensions of a painting's surface. Cubism sought to replace the representational system of one-point perspective with an altogether different system that had the ability to depict an object from more than one point of view simultaneously. In this respect, the Cubists attempted to introduce the aspect of time into their static depiction of reality. Ordinarily, paintings had depicted a person or object frozen in time—the viewer could only see the subject from one side or angle. With the perspective system, the only way to depict an object from multiple angles was to do it sequentially, such as is done in the cinema.

Cubism attempted to synthesize many views of an object into one painting. When this was done on a simple scale, the unity of

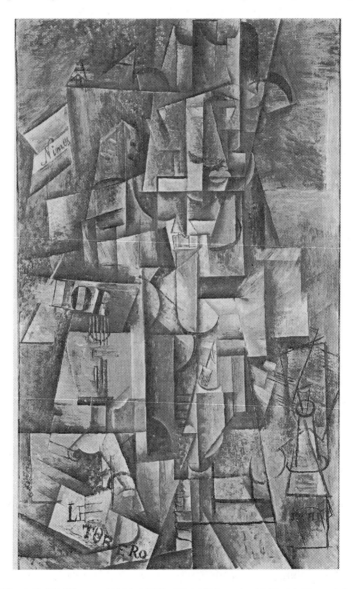

Fig. 1: Pablo Picasso (1881–1973). *The Aficionado,* 1912. (c) Copyright ARS, New York. Kunstmuseum, Basel, Switzerland. Giraudon/Art Resource, New York.

the object could be more or less retained. But when this was done with the complexity of *The Aficionado*, it resulted in fragmented chaos.

With this background in mind, let us consider the "structural" principles applicable to this problem, namely the general character of reality that is presented in the Bible. For the Christian, our understanding of the basic character or nature of reality is derived from the doctrine of the creation. Genesis 1 teaches us that the creation, as it was originally brought into being out of nothing by God, was "formless and empty." It was essentially an empty, chaotic, amorphous, watery "deep" which God subsequently, through the actions of filling and separating (making distinctions), made into the ordered, beautifully designed reality we now know and enjoy. This is another way in which creation reflects the character of God who is "not a God of disorder but of peace" (1 Cor. 14:33).

Furthermore, the Bible reveals that the peaceful harmony and unity of the creation is continually held together by Christ (Col. 1:17). We therefore conclude that reality, as created and continually governed by God, is orderly, unified and harmonious, yet is made up of discreet objects and creatures that in themselves have integrity, an inner harmony and unity. Any artwork which attempts to depict reality then, if consonant with the Scripture's teachings, should reflect this understanding of reality.

Returning to Picasso, we can see in the case of *The Aficionado* that the subject—a man reading a newspaper—is dealt with in such a way that the integrity and inner unity of the subject is lost. In this respect it runs entirely counter to the biblical understanding of the character of reality. Even though Picasso gives us a great deal of information on the subject presented (no doubt one familiar with this kind of radical Cubism could decipher and interpret its jumble of parts), this cacophony of data is so arbitrarily synthesized as to completely break down the harmony and unity of the original subject and thereby throw the viewer into a state of confusion. Furthermore, the composition of the painting is itself lacking unity and order. A feeble attempt at unity is made by using a narrow range of colors. It would seem then that in this extreme form of Cubism, the "structure" of the original subject is so completely ignored, abrogated, or suppressed as to leave virtually nothing for the Christian painter to redeem.

The prognosis of *Mandolin and Guitar* is somewhat better. In this case, while Picasso uses the devices of distortion and simplification quite freely, the integrity and unity of the original parts is maintained. One can clearly distinguish patterned tablecloth from yellow and black mandolin and white, red, and brown

Fig. 2: Pablo Picasso. *Mandolin and Guitar*, 1924. Oil with sand on canvas, 55 3/8 x 78 7/8 inches. Solomon R. Guggenheim Museum, New York. Photo by David Heald (c)The Solomon R. Guggenheim Foundation, New York. (FN 53. 1358)

guitar; tile floor from opened balcony window and shutter in the background. The question for us here is about the use of exaggeration and simplification in many forms. It is not in itself bad or evil. But how far is too far? A general rule might be that distortion is lawful when it is used in a constructive, non-disparaging manner that still maintains the integrity of the original. I think that in the case of *Mandolin and Guitar*, there is a great deal for the Christian artist to plunder lawfully. There is a kind of jazzy, playful, joyous atmosphere in this work which, for a legitimate subject matter, would be a most appropriate stylistic vehicle. Here, as in all cases, the Christian would have to use decorum. This style would not be suited to a portrait of Grandma, for instance. But the style of *Mandolin and Guitar* in many respects could be redeemed.

The fourth and final ingredient in the reclamation process that I wish to highlight is the cultivation of an appropriate attitude. Although I am sure that additional aspects or a correct attitude could be examined, I have isolated three which I think are crucial.

First, we need to approach non-Christian art with an air of sobriety. This means that we execute the task of critiquing art with "fear and trembling," with alertness and seriousness. Just as idols posed a threat to the covenant obedience of the ancient Israelites, so contemporary non-Christian art poses a real danger to our spiritual welfare. Of course, in dealing with the world around us, we have more freedom than the Jews of the OT. But our freedom in Christ is never a license to sin. A flippant attitude can lead to ruin.

Second, we need patience and perseverance. Analyzing the structure and direction of artworks in the light of Scripture takes time and effort. Assimilating the results of our critical research will also be a gradual process. We must therefore guard against being too hasty, being too quick to accept the latest in fashion, or jumping on the contemporary artistic bandwagon. We must be disciplined, persevere, and be faithful to God in our critical and artistic tasks, rather than striving after success and acceptance by the standards of the world.

Third, we need to take on artistic and critical tasks with passion. By this, I do not mean blind, unbridled emotion or sheer exuberance. Rather, I am speaking of a deep concern about what we are doing: self-consciously serving and loving Christ, our Master in heaven, as we carry out our tasks here on earth. We must do nothing less than an excellent job in our evaluation of non-Christian art, receiving strength from God to complete each task well.

In conclusion, I want to make two further points. First, although we can and should legitimately plunder the contemporary non-Christian artistic riches we find around us in the cautious manner I have described, we should not forget the vast Christian cultural heritage that is behind us. Our artistic forefathers have left us excellent painting, music, drama, and literature from which we can learn and borrow—not to mention the art of the Bible itself! Please don't think I am advocating the slavish copying or mimicking of Christian styles from the past. There needs to be progress, a respectful updating of the splendors of the past.

We need to develop a sense of our place in history. It is easy to look at the woeful artistic conditions of the Church today and sing a continual lament. But I want to leave you with a sense of the excitement and hope I see in our present situation. In the times of Ezra, Haggai, and Zechariah, there was a similar pall of despair and hopelessness. The beloved temple of Solomon lay in ruins, leveled by the Chaldeans some fifty years before. But this situation became the occasion for the building of a new temple, more beautiful and splendid than the first. So I see our situation today. The Church's artistic life lies in ruin. But this provides present-day Christians with the opportunity to build it anew, to undo the mistakes we have made in the past, and to establish an artistic milieu entirely founded on biblical principles. By forming and following a thoroughly Christian vision for the arts, we might have the privilege to see this dream become a reality.

SUGGESTED READING

The following books and articles are recommended for further study on the topics covered in this book. Many of these works were profoundly influential on me as I formed my views on culture. Those marked with a "†" are deemed most important for the development of a biblical understanding of culture.

Bavinck, Herman. "Calvin and Common Grace" in *Calvin and the Reformation*, edited by William Park Armstrong. Grand Rapids, MI: Baker, 1980. Reprint of 1909 ed.

Eliot, T.S. *Christianity and Culture: The Idea of a Christian Society and Notes Towards the Definition of Culture.* New York: Harcourt, Brace & World, 1960. †

Meeter, H. Henry. *The Basic Ideas of Calvinism.* 5th rev. ed. Grand Rapids, MI: Kregel, 1956.

Murray, John. "Common Grace" in *Collected Writings of John Murray.* Vol. 2. Carlisle, PA: Banner of Truth, 1976–82.

Myers, Kenneth A. *All God's Children and Blue Suede Shoes: Christians & Popular Culture.* Westchester, IL: Crossway, 1989.

Niebuhr, H. Richard. *Christ and Culture.* New York: Harper & Row, 1951. †

Schilder, Klaas. *Christ and Culture.* Winnipeg: Premier, 1977.

Van Til, Henry R. *The Calvinistic Concept of Culture.* Grand Rapids, MI: Baker, 1959. †

Wolters, Albert M. *Creation Regained: Biblical Basics for a Reformational Worldview.* Grand Rapids, MI: Eerdmans, 1985. †

Scripture Index

Subject/Author Index